Heartbeat Ni ...py

Healing Our Hearts

A Guide for Friends and Lovers

By
Amara Karuna

Karuna Publishing © 2011
Pahoa, HI

Dedicated to my parents, Richard and Jane

ISBN 0-9842274-4-X
EAN-13 978-0-9842274-4-0

Heartbeat Nurturing Therapy

Published by
KARUNA PUBLISHING
PO BOX 1430
PAHOA HI 96778
www.karunapublishing.com
See also www.karunaarts.com

Publication: July 2011 by Karuna Publishing
Copyright © 2011 by Amara Karuna All rights reserved
Cover design by Amara Karuna
Photography and design by Amara Karuna.

First Karuna Publishing Paperback Printing:

July 2011
10 9 8 7 6 5 4 3 2 1

What People Say:

"Taking the Heartbeat Nurturing Therapy class was a profound experience in and of itself. It caused such a degree of de-armoring, of "getting real," that it took my whole life and forced the moment to its crisis, so to speak. It laid bare whatever was not working authentically and also what was authentically true about me and my life. In less than 24 hours my vision, being so cleared, produced the action steps that provide the context for my destiny, if you will. All the pieces fell into place perfectly and my understanding, too. It was so fast and amazing as to feel miraculous. I feel blessed by your presence and your class. "
    I. H, Seattle, WA

"I'm excited that I have now perspective enough to see how the emotions that come up for me are arrows pointing to the places I need healing, and I'm eager to love those hurts and grow from that. So, overall I'm feeling freer and bigger and more peaceful and so deeply grateful that I cry (I think sorrow also for all the times I haven't loved myself) as I write this to you. You and your life and what you bring are a big gift and an inspiration to me. And proof to me that a life of love is possible and yummy and attainable."
    M. G. Pahoa, HI

"The work I have done with Amara has had a deep, profound impact on my life. I am so grateful to have her skilled and graceful guidance in exploring the potentially uncomfortable and mysterious terrain of both my mind and body. The heightened awareness and self-knowledge I have gained is life changing and empowering."
    L. C. Hilo, HI

Table of Contents

Introduction

I began working with my early memories of infancy and birth because of symptoms of physical pain that were long term and chronic, and were seriously blocking my ability to function and enjoy life. I learned peer counseling in my 20's and it has been a wonderful help all my adult life. I learned to focus on the earliest memories in counseling, to get the most effectiveness from my sessions, because those early imprints form the root of all later issues.

I began to experience physical sensations and feelings arising from my body during sessions, and images of my experiences of birth and pre-birth. Although I knew that everything we have experienced is recorded somewhere in our brain, I thought it was not possible to remember such early moments. But there they were, clear and strong. I felt feelings of my heart and neck being pushed and compressed, and feelings of the numbness and disassociation typical of anesthesia. My body was shaking and moving of its own accord. Deep feelings of vulnerability and fearful shock, and also abandonment came through and released as tears and sounds.

Always after these sessions, I felt a renewed energy and different perspective on life. When I discovered that being held and role-playing the early events increased the effectiveness, I used many of my sessions doing that technique. Gradually over time, my persistent fear of the physical world and reluctance to be embodied have been fading and changing to joy and peace in being alive. Also my personal intimate relationships have shifted from being full of fear, control and attachment to much more love, freedom and personal empowerment.

Heartbeat Nurturing Therapy addresses the pain that many of us experienced as infants in our birth process, and also the lack of skin contact and breastfeeding from our mothers after birth. Our birth is the primal imprint, the initiation moment on which we base our beliefs about life. Unsatisfied needs for oral stimulation and closeness can lead to overeating, smoking, relationship problems and other addictions later in life.

In this form of therapy we can offer new imprints of love and nurturance directly back to those younger parts of ourselves. This frees us to create more mature and satisfying intimate contacts with others.

This book outlines a simple and deeply therapeutic practice that can be done with friends or lovers, or as a solo practice by yourself. It is a way of loving yourself and others deeply; reaching into areas of the most basic infantile needs and giving nurturing. Since the practice is so simple, anyone can do it, and people can easily exchange sessions with each other as a conscious form of nurturing and sharing.

Within a spiritual and intentional context, we act as healing channels to help release this pain and create new healthy imprints in the psyche. A version of inner child therapy, this process works with accessing the infant self and memories still stored in our deep subconscious and cellular memory. By using ritual, hypnotic induction, massage, touch, sound and spoken words, we open a direct channel back to that time and those experiences around birth. We seek to fill some of the unmet needs of that time, and create new and healthier imprints and neural pathways.

This book is intended as a basic introduction to some ideas and practices that can be deeply satisfying and healing when trading therapy with friends and lovers. I use the words "counselor", "therapist" and "giver" interchangeably in this book, and these terms do not imply any level of training.

You may have many of these skills already, and be able to skip through a lot of the chapters. If you are completely new to any of this, then give yourself a while to learn and practice, and don't expect to do it perfectly at the beginning. Making mistakes is part of the learning process. Do be aware that this is a powerful therapy technique that can and probably will bring up deep and old issues. Get support from experienced counselors if you run into problems.

Professionals may find this technique to be useful and integrate it into their practice, if they are free to actually be physically close to their clients. A person trained to give these sessions is affectionately called a Mamadevi or Papadeva, (Sanscrit: deva means diety) and they may offer these as part of a tantric healing ministry or as a part of being a sexual surrogate. Often this is prohibited by law for professionals, since they risk their clients becoming confused with transference (attachment), or feelings of being sexually abused. This technique is most effective and least confusing when done between people who are trusting of each other, and not exchanging money for the service.

This is not a thorough guide to all the details of working with the emotions that may arise while doing therapy. Each chapter could be expanded to its own book, since the topics are so broad. I will give you an outline of the basic technique, and ideas for several ways to use it, as well as the background skills needed to use the full technique.

Information has been included on many relevant topics, with ideas about how to approach them therapeutically. We will explore the need for healing and the negative effects of common western birth procedures. For those who are new to therapy or counseling, the basics of how to do emotional release work, peer counseling, inner child work and role-playing are explored. You'll find an explanation of the process of deep relaxation, hypnotic induction and regression, and spiritual invocation.

Various practices are recommended in learning these processes, and each one is highlighted so you can easily find them. The practices can be done in pairs or on your own in many cases. If you are interested in learning more about the skills involved in any of these, see the Resources section.

This book assumes that if you are practicing giving this therapy, you feel that you are able to hold loving space for another person to go into and through some very strong feelings. This service can have very lasting and profound effects on the lives of those who receive it. I hope you practice this and teach it and share it widely, because now we need all the love and nurturing we can create to spread out blessings through our world.

May you know deep peace within.

Amara Wahaba Karuna

With deep gratitude

for all my wonderful teachers

all my family

all my counselors

and all my students and friends

You are always in my heart

Chapter 1.
Humans and Emotions

What happens when we decide to be partners and build family with someone, and after a few months or years the rosy glow of our idealism wears off and it seems to become so much more difficult than we imagined? Why do we find ourselves arguing, feeling jealous, greedy, and uncooperative? It seems if the other person would just do it our way, and stop being so unreasonable, things would work out great!

How do we communicate what we want without being controlling? How do we stay connected when our needs seem to be conflicting with others? Why do we keep trying to stop drinking, smoking or eating too much, and find it such an ongoing struggle? Why does life seem so unsatisfying at times?

Emotional problems between people are the main reason for breaking up relationships, businesses and communities. Because our Western culture is so emotionally repressed, most people have no models for how to handle their own emotions in a responsible and healthy way. We go through life hoping for peace and pleasure, and if we get triggered or have our "buttons pushed", we tend to blow up out of control, and then try to get out of the unpleasant emotions as fast as possible, without really understanding where they came from or why they are so intense.

The shadow is any part of the psyche that is unpopular and judged as undesirable. Shadows exist because of an accumulation of past hurtful experiences. We can see our own shadows in the places where we find ourselves compulsively doing things that we have already decided we do not want to do, such as indulging in addictions. It is also seen in chronic illnesses that we can't seem to heal. Or where we feel blocked in moving forward toward the things we want to create in our lives.

Shadows live in our unconscious, so by their nature they are hard to see. It is far easier to notice something you do not like about another person, thus projecting your shadow on to them. The problem with shadows is that no matter what attempts are made to control or ignore them, they keep popping their ugly little heads up in the most inopportune and embarrassing moments.

This is because they want healing, and they want to be honored and acknowledged. The longer they are pushed away and repressed, the more energy they build up, until they really seem like monsters lurking somewhere under the thin veneer of our "nice" conscious personalities.

The good news is that shadows and old emotional distresses can be cleared and permanently resolved, with loving help from others. This book is intended as a resource for people who would like to help themselves, their friends and their lovers to feel more deeply satisfied with life and relationships.

This chapter and the next give a summary of some of the basic ideas from Re-evaluation Co-counseling (RC), because it is a really

2

useful groundwork on which to base our more specific Heartbeat Nurturing Therapy. If you have not yet been trained as a co-counselor, these chapters are important.

What is Peer Counseling, and Why Do It?

Peer counseling is aimed at teaching lay people how to be effective in helping themselves and others with emotional issues, and in regaining our innate goodness and intelligence. It is based on observation of what really works in practice, not on theories of what ought to work. It evolved from the experiences of thousands of people.

You can use it on different levels. Some people have sessions occasionally just to blow off steam in stressful times. Some set up regular sessions which provide a deep long term therapy, systematically removing the blocks that keep them from realizing their dreams.

Re-evaluation Co-counseling is a world wide network of non-professional counselors, who trade sessions for the purpose of clearing emotions, dissolving rigid patterns of behavior and recovering the ability to be present and think clearly and rationally. It is a people's liberation movement that started in the 60's and has spread all over the world. RC has spawned many permutations and offshoots, such as Co-Counseling International, the National Coalition Building Institute, and Wholistic Peer Support Counseling.

This spreading of information was encouraged by Harvey Jackins, the founder of RC, because of his generous attitude that the more people who know and practice their own healing, the faster the world situation will improve. You can see the original organization at www.rc.org, where you will find many resources for learning the skills.

Human Nature and Intelligence

What are human beings really like? Underneath all the programs, conditioning, expectations and hurts that we get, what is our true basic nature? Think about: What would you be like if you were really free to be your true self? What are young children like before they are socialized?

Human beings are basically intelligent, zestful, loving, communicative and cooperative. We love to be close with each other, and we love to share. We love to create things. Our inherent nature has a vast capacity for flexible intelligence. Each of us is whole and complete, unique, and with limitless potential. Nothing can permanently damage our real nature, but many things can cover it up.

3

When our thinking process is working well, when we are relaxed and feeling normal, information from our environment comes in mostly on a subconscious level. Most of what is happening at any time does not need our conscious attention, such as sounds sights, smells, temperature of the air, etc. It gets evaluated, processed and sorted, and then filed in our memory to be recalled at will later. We can respond to each new situation with an appropriate, new and creative response.

How We Get Hurt

Why don't people always act according to our true inner nature? If we are so cooperative and loving, why are we killing each other and the planet? Through the natural process of living, we get hurt. We get hurt physically, mentally and emotionally on all levels, and frequently. This is a normal part of life, and we are equipped to deal with it, if we were allowed to.

When we are being hurt, our thinking process shuts down, or seems to work very differently. People do not usually think well while hurting. The forebrain, which holds the more evolved part of our brain and the capacity for rational thought, becomes less dominant. The more primitive reptilian brain area takes over, inducing feelings of fight or flight. Did you ever try to think or make decisions with a headache or while you are very upset?

The input of information from the environment is still pouring in, but it's not getting processed or evaluated as usual, and a kind of mis-storage occurs. All the sights, sounds, smells, etc., emotions, as well as the experience of being unable to think clearly get stuck together in one big recording/memory. This recording is like a videotape of the incident, which is stored for later processing, perhaps at a safer time.

Emotions are natural waves of energy that arise in response to a stimulus, and if they are allowed to flow and are not repressed, they naturally resolve themselves. It is natural for a child to get angry if another child steals a toy, or if they are denied a food that they really want. The emotion can be validated and allowed space to be felt, and yet not be the deciding factor in how the situation is resolved.

Hurtful things happen to us as a natural part of life, and our emotional responses to them are our natural way of healing the hurts. A child who is sad about not having another cookie can be allowed to cry, and have the feeling acknowledged in a respectful way. They can be given empathy, but not another cookie, and soon the tears will wash through and the inner sun with shine again.

4

In our lives, in this culture, we experience many disappoint-ments and moments of neglect, abuse and not having our needs met. If we are not given loving empathetic attention around the emotions stirred by these hurts, they tend to get stored in our subconscious shadows. In an ideal situation, as soon as the hurtful event is over, the person would be able to release the hurt and heal. Hurts always naturally seek release. However the safe space, time, and attention from a caring person that encourages the healing are not usually available to most of us, so the emotions and information tends to stay stuck. They will stay stuck an entire lifetime unless they are processed.

A stored hurt creates a rigid, inflexible spot in our mind, a recording of the whole event. The recording seems to take up space, to use up some of our capacity for intelligence. All the information seems to be stored in one big lump, like a recorded movie. Separate bits can't be remembered individually as they can when it is stored normally. It becomes a place where we can't think well, that when alone we avoid remembering.

Why? What happens right now when you think about something that was really a hurtful event? You re-experience the hurt. It's all still right there, and so we try to avoid remembering it.

Practice: Scan Your Triggers
Take a moment and think of times when you have acted like that. Maybe write them down for further reflection. This behavior indicates a place here you have been hurt, and still carry the scars of that hurt.

The recordings wait in our subconscious storage vault, like a booby trap. When anything later happens which is similar enough to the original hurts, we experience that unpleasant phenomenon known as being triggered. The new situation may not even be a hurtful event. It may just be similar in any way to the old event. We call this being "Re-stimulated" or "Triggered." It's also commonly known as getting your buttons pushed, or overreacting. When the old recording starts to play, it feels like a replaying of the old incident. You feel the same feelings, find your self saying the same words or compulsively doing the same actions. It takes you out of the present and into the past.

A person acting out of an old distress recording will say things that are not pertinent, do things that don't work, and fail to cope effectively and gracefully with the present situation. They will feel terrible feelings that may have nothing to do with the present situation.

5

You can tell you've come across residue in someone because they're acting frozen, nonsensical or rigid. They become irrational and "not themselves". They may get memory flashes of the old situation. "Temporary insanity" is a classic description of being triggered.

Whenever someone is triggered, and they have failed to cope effectively with the new situation, it also becomes a new hurtful experience. It gets recorded with all its new feelings, sensations and thoughts. Thus new situations are added on top of the old ones, and the distress recording gets bigger, adding more layers.

This means the booby trap has more triggers. It takes up more of our free thinking space, and there are less areas of experience in life that are not upsetting to us. The person becomes more disposed to be upset by more situations, and more deeply upset, and for longer times.

We get hurt early and often. We get hurt by accident when we are babies; we get bumps, or get cold, hungry, frustrated or scared. This could get taken care of by our inherent healing process, if it were allowed to happen. But by far the greatest cause of our hurts is from contagion from irrational adults. For example, when a child runs outside naked, and the parent (having been punished by their own parents for exactly the same thing) gets upset and yells at the child, telling them how bad and embarrassing they have been acting. Then the child carries guilt, shame and fear about their body as a distress.

When there has been enough re-stimulation, and when the same hurts happen over and over, they form patterns, which become incorporated into our personalities and even reflected in our body structure. They color our beliefs and effect every part of our lives.

Most patterns are latent, when you do not feel the distress all the time, but it lies inside waiting to be pulled out by a similar event. We see these as our "problems". We know that we get triggered by certain things. "Oh, I always get mad when someone is late for anything." "I hate to talk in front of a group".

Practice: Scan Your Beliefs About the World

What kinds of chronic patterns have you seen in yourself and others? Take a moment and write down the basic ideas about life and this world that you base your actions on. What do you believe about yourself? About the world?

Chronic patterns are created when we are hurt so frequently over a long time, that the feelings become pervasive, and we think

6

"that's just the way I am". These are seen as idiosyncrasies of personality, or as your viewpoint on reality. Chronic patterns are constantly triggered; they play all the time. They are like colored glasses through which we see the world. They can be identified in a person's posture, speech, emotional attitudes (like pessimism), and ritual rigid behaviors (like compulsions and addictions).

The Natural Healing Process

The process of storing hurts can be reversed. Our abilities to think clearly and respond freely can be recovered, and repaired. A natural healing process is built in, and we are all born with it. If it could operate, it would allow stored distress to be removed immediately. This emotional release process can be called "discharge" in the sense of discharging or draining a battery, or catharsis.

Emotional release is a natural, inherent process. Every young child does it spontaneously. It is a physical, chemical process that happens in our bodies. When sad, we naturally cry and sob. When afraid, we laugh, tremble and have cold sweat. When angry we rage with loud sounds and large movements, and have hot sweat. When we have physical discomfort we relieve it by yawning and stretching. When we want to communicate an experience we do so with animated, non-repetitive talking. All of these are avenues of release for the emotional energy, and have a healing effect if done consciously within a safe and loving situation, with someone who wants to listen.

If the process of catharsis is allowed to finish, the stuck information in the distress recording is released, evaluated and stored correctly. The area of our thinking around the old painful moment is restored to flexible awareness. This is called "Re-evaluation," and is an automatic response after emotion has been discharged. It is the "Aha" feeling of resolution and understanding that comes after releasing. The purpose of counseling is to encourage the catharsis process so that we can reclaim all the areas of our flexible thinking that have been blocked.

Blocks to the Healing Process

What keeps the natural healing process from happening?

Originally it is the lack of an attentive, loving person at the moment of the hurtful experience. In painful moments, we are often alone or the others around are involved somehow in their own pain. There is a vast shortage of people who know how to truly pay attention to someone else when they are hurting.

7

We grow up with a chronic feeling of never having enough personal attention. This is due to similar hurts instilled in the adults we depend on, and also to the isolating structure of our society, which makes it very hard for parents to get the help they need. Do you feel like you got enough attention while growing up?

Our culture also confuses the healing process with the hurt. We think if someone is crying, we need to get them to stop, and then they will be all better. We do not realize that the crying itself was what would make the hurt dissolve.

Inhibitions are learned early. We are told "don't cry", and get lots of patting, rocking, threats, or humiliation: "Big boys don't cry". Or "I'll give you something to cry about." Soon the inhibitions become internalized, and we stop ourselves without having to be told.

No form of catharsis is more important than the others. If they are encouraged and persisted with, the stuck hurt will be released in just the right way for the client. Often you will have many different feelings about one hurtful event.

Everyone keeps trying to get attention, although not with awareness. We talk out our problems, or cry on a shoulder with friends. If you listen, much of everyday conversation is people trying to client about their problems. But it is hard to be thorough and deep with this unaware "clienting", because our conditioning not to have feelings takes over whenever the discharge gets deep. Also friends are often unskilled at listening and will often offer advice, give criticism, or just take the attention back to themselves by interrupting and talking about their own feelings.

In co-counseling we structure our time together so that we create a safe time for us each to have a turn being listened to, when the listener has been trained to listen well. In this way deep and true healing can take place. In Heartbeat Therapy, we do some of this discussion and listening work before and after the cradling sessions, so it is useful to know the skills.

If the discharge process is allowed to operate, people can return to natural state of freedom and zestful living. Each gain in recovering our capacity for intelligence is worthwhile, even if it is small.

Chronic Isolation and Fear of Intimacy

One of the main things that keeps all the emotional patterning in place is the isolation that is built in to our modern society. We have gotten far away from our tribal roots, and many people live alone, or in small families. Our daily lives are not structured to create opportunities for deep sharing and closeness.

Most people hope to find one other person to live and be partners with. They depend on that one person for all their needs for sharing and intimacy. Even if we do have a partner, the internal and external stresses often make it hard to have enough satisfying time together. As we can see, this places great stress on the primary relationship, and many relationships do not last long. The feelings of hurt and rejection are added to old feelings, until a fear of any intimacy arises. It seems easier just to be alone. Many people struggle just to have any closeness and connection in their lives.

When we take time to share therapeutic time in sessions, it creates an opportunity to not only release our programs about isolation, but to meet some of our actual needs for closeness. By going to the roots of our first experiences of closeness in infancy, we create a situation where the patterns can be re-structured.

Chapter 2.
How We Can Help Each Other

How To Begin As A Counselor

Mostly in Heartbeat Therapy sessions, we use only listening with loving attention, and non-verbal sounds. The only spoken words from the therapist during a session are the messages that the client has said they want to hear. The giver plays the role of the loving parent, and the receiver becomes the child or infant.

Before and after the session, we will use more discussion, and for these parts it is good to understand permissive counseling. In these parts of the session, the setting is two adults relating as equals. There are certain ways of listening and asking questions that will be more successful and helpful, and certain things to avoid doing.

Begin by giving the receiver your complete, aware attention. Listen with interest and full attention. Ideally be relaxed, cheerful, confident and loving. This is healing all by itself, and is a remedy to basic hurts of not getting enough attention. This can go a long way, even if you do nothing else.

Attention from another person is a tangible gift of energy exchange, that is why it is called "giving attention". Make sure you are in a good space and have attention to give. If not, get some help for yourself first. The giver should maintain eye contact, while the receiver may, or may not as they choose.

Practice: The Counselor's Attitude

Look at someone without any conversation, just in silence, and imagine looking under the mask of who they think they are. Look at the real human underneath with an attitude of respect. Keep in mind that they are fully powerful, capable humans, who may have just forgotten this momentarily. They will solve their own problems, and they just need your attention and support to do so. You don't have to figure it out for them. They have always done their best.   Accept them just as they are, and generate an attitude of loving kindness.

Any difficulty in keeping this attitude will show where your own patterns are hidden. Whenever anyone is upset, this attitude from you will be of great help to them.

Creating Safety

Be respectful of your counselor's gift of attention to you. Just because they have given you a great session one day, does not mean they will now be available to you at any moment you need help. Ask them each time if they are willing to give a session.   Be able to hear a "no" in a graceful way. Don't just start talking about the things you are disturbed about with out permission. It takes energy to hear about someone's pain. Be sure to give back to them equally, so that you are not setting up a one way dependence.   Make sure you have clear agreements about how long the session will last, and stick to them.

In general, be courteous, arrive on time, and be responsible about rescheduling if need be. Make the environment safe; no phone calls, no distractions and no children or pets wanting attention. Do whatever is needed to ensure privacy and comfort. Decide who goes first by checking in about who feels they need it most. Or flip a coin.

Do not break or harm anything that is valuable, or disrupt the environment with inappropriate noise (be aware of muffling sounds if there are nearby neighbors). Don't come under the influence of drugs, ideally even caffeine and sugar. Strong chemicals interfere with the natural ability to release and change the hormonal balance.

At the end of a session, make sure to bring the receiver back to this moment. Help them come back out of their feelings into normal awareness. The moments after a session are important to help them close the door to the old feelings and continue on with the rest of their day. People can be assisted in this by talking about things that are pleasant and neutral, or by moving around physically. Direct them to look around the room and find something interesting to discuss, or ask them about their favorite book or movie.

Confidentiality: Avoid referring to anything from the session after it ends, as this may bring up the feelings again. This is especially important if you are giving to a partner.

If the client feels still upset after a session, it probably means you did not spend enough time getting the attention out of the past, or that the issue you were working with needs more time in session to come to a sense of resolution. They can work with more attention outs, or do a little journaling to help process what they felt.

Practice: Listening Well
In pairs, listen to another person with full attention and without adding anything but short, one word comments, for 5 minutes. Trade. Discussion afterward: What was hard or easy about that? Do not discuss what was said, but only the process.

Things to keep in mind as the counselor:

The healing process of emotional release is natural. Do not confuse the healing process with the actual hurt. Many people do this, believing that if they can stop the releasing, then the hurt will be gone. It only goes underneath to wait for another time. The tears are not the grief; they are the natural way of releasing the grief. Trembling is not the terror; it is the release of terror. If they are all encouraged and persisted with, the stuck hurt will be released in just the right way for the client.

What to Do As A Counselor

Permissive Counseling

Permissive counseling is best used when first learning to counsel, and when starting with a new client you are unfamiliar with. It is good when counseling children, or people (like friends or relatives) who are not trained as peer counselors, and who might not welcome more active guidance.

It's better to be silent if you're not sure what to say.

In permissive counseling, the therapist becomes a little more active than just listening. Now you may ask questions and make short comments for two reasons:

1. To reassure them of your interest and validate their feelings.

Examples:
Client: "I can barely stand to think about that, it was so painful."
Counselor: "That incident really hurt you a lot." (Paraphrasing)

Client: "I've never been able to admit this to anyone before."
Counselor: "Thank you for trusting me with it. I appreciate your bravery in doing it now." (Giving appreciation)

Client: "I don't think I am doing this very well. I am just boring you."
Counselor: ""I really do want to hear all about this. This is really hard stuff you are working on. You are doing just fine." (Validation)

Client: "I know I shouldn't be angry, but it really bothered me!"
Counselor: "You have a right to feel whatever is real for you." Or "It's fine to let that anger be there." (Permission to feel)

2. To steer and guide their attention back to feelings, and draw them out. Notice what ideas or feelings bring release and dwell on that. Support the way they want to go.

Examples:

Client: "And then he had the nerve to tell me it was all my fault!"
Counselor: "What did you want to say to him them?" (Leading questions)

Client: "And then my dad yelled at me and told me to stay in my room."
Counselor: "What was your experience of that?" or "How was that for you?" "What did you feel then?" (Drawing out the feeling)

Client: "I can't think of anything to talk about right now."
Counselor: "What was the last thing that really bothered you?" or "Tell me your life story" or "Is there anything you would like to change in your life?" (Scanning the past, free association)

Client: "And then my best friend dumped me, and I felt really helpless and afraid to talk to anyone."
Counselor: "Have similar things happened to you in the past? When was that?" (This helps to get to the early root of a problem)

What Not To Do As A Counselor

Avoid giving advice: "You should really have told him off!" "I handled that problem by..." Allow them to work out their own unique solutions to their own unique problems. Even if they ask you "What should I do?" turn it back around to them by asking "What do you think?" or "If I were you, what advice would you give me?" or "I can't know what is best for you. I trust you to figure this out."

Avoid being judgmental or invalidating: "Why did you let her treat you like that?" or "Aren't you over-reacting?" or "Oh you don't need to be upset by that little thing!"

Avoid talking about your own experiences, such as similar problems, during their time. This takes the attention off them and easily leads to giving advice or unaware clienting. "I know just how you feel, the exact same thing happened to me!" "My dad always did that, too."

Avoid sympathizing with an "Oh poor you" attitude. "You poor thing, that is awful!" Compassion for the client's experience can happen while still respecting their true, powerful inner nature.

Avoid reacting emotionally. Indifference, hostility, sadness or other strong emotion from you will not be helpful. You can sometimes release some along with the client, like laughing and a few tears, but only if you can do it less that they are and keep your attention on them. If you can't, you need to stop the session and do something to restore your attention.

Do not interrupt emotional release. If someone is in the middle of laughing, crying, or otherwise expressing emotion, do not interfere. Wait until there is a slackening of catharsis before you make additional comments.

Avoid being suggestive and giving opinions. Don't tell them what you think of their problem. "I think that is terrible! He should be fired for that." "You boyfriend is really treating you badly."

Avoid putting words into a client's mouth, or suggesting how they may be feeling: "It seems like you wish you could get back at her." Better just to ask: "How do you feel?"

Avoid making connections for a client, like pointing out the similarities between incidents and material: "Oh, that is just like when you father and mother left you alone before." Or "Doesn't that remind you of your father and mother?" Instead ask them what it reminds them of.

Do not ask irrelevant questions just to satisfy your own curiosity. It doesn't really matter if you know all the details. "When was your uncle in England?"

Avoid interpreting, or analyzing, such as "perhaps she did that because she felt insecure." Or "You probably felt that way because your Mom never held you." "Maybe that bothered you because..." Stick with feeling the feelings.

Avoid oppressive jokes, or teasing comments that put people down or belittle them. To create safety, we need to give each other complete respect.

What Not To Do As A Client

It is useful to avoid certain topics, especially as a beginning student, in order to help your peer counselor give you good attention. Some topics are generally hard for most people to listen to, and it is best to avoid them, at least in the beginning. They can sometimes be worked on later, when the counselor is more skilled and experienced, or with other counselors.

Avoid referring to what the other person said when it was their turn as a client. "When you were talking about how your uncle beat you up, I really felt bad for you." "I know what you mean about how stupid schools are. They treated me the same way." This is especially common when it is your turn to go second as a client. This brings up their material again and makes it hard for them to listen well to you. Stick to your own experiences and memories, even if they are similar.

Avoid talking about your feelings about oppressed groups (women, people of color, elders, gays and lesbians, etc.) with a counselor who is a member of that group, unless you are also in that group. In other words, don't talk about how angry you are at women with a woman, unless you are also a woman. It would be better for a man with these feelings to discuss it with another man. Don't talk about how much you love black culture with a black person, unless you are also black. Choose people in other groups to tell.

Avoid talking about your feelings, opinions and judgments about your counselor's life and personality. "I'm really attracted to you." "How can you live in this dump?" This is usually very hard for people to listen to. If something really needs to be cleared, do it in a three way session or a relationship session, not while they are trying to be your therapist.

Avoid talking about your feelings, opinions and judgments about any of the counselor's close friends or family. "Your girlfriend is really sexy!" "I know you are friends with Mary, but I hate how she whines all the time." The listener will have trouble staying neutral.

Practice: Short Sessions

With a partner, listen to them attentively for 5 or 10 minutes, asking questions and making comments as described above. Then take a moment to get their attention back to present, by looking at things in the room or moving around a bit. Ask them what you did

well, and if there is anything you could have done differently as a counselor. This feedback helps you learn.
Then trade roles.

Rewriting the Programs

The old patterns have a strong pull to keep things the same old way, yet they can be reprogrammed, just like a computer. When the person is invited to explore past memories, and sink back into old feelings, it opens a metaphorical doorway into the past. Then the past painful memories can be acknowledged, honored, explored and can be re-written. When the healing loving presence of another being is added to the old story, it creates new neural connections in the brain. The story can be told again, the way it could have been. This is one of the most powerful and effective therapeutic techniques, and it is what Heartbeat Therapy is based on.

There are many books currently written on the new science that studies how the brain works and can be programmed. Studies show that when someone experiences something such as watching a movie, their brain reacts to the storyline as though it is really happening. All the inner chemistry, muscle contractions, hormonal and brainwave changes happen as though you are an actor in the drama. This makes visualization and role-playing therapies very powerful for writing a new script on which to base our beliefs and behavior.

Counteraction

A counteraction (in RC known as contradictions) is anything that is different enough from the old distress that it helps the person see beyond that old reality. It can be anything that is different from the way we were hurt. It is like a remedy, or a medicine that soothes the pain or fills the need that was not filled.

The most important basic passive counteractions are listening and touch. There are no old pain recordings that include having someone listen well and lovingly to our feelings. If that had happened, the pain would not still be recorded! Also, holding hands and other loving touch is a usually a good counteraction, since this was not usually happening when the person was being hurt.

We also use the affirmations or messages during Heartbeat Therapy, as sweet loving words that a parent would speak to a cherished child. These are designed by the client in advance, so the therapist knows what will be most satisfying for them to hear. When you find one that evokes catharsis, **repeat it** until the release slackens, and then you can try to modify the direction to provide a more accurate counteraction. This process "milks" the stuck emotion out of that area, and eventually cleans it up. If the release process stops when a new message is given, go back to what worked before.

When Emotions Let Go

Emotional release is not something you can make happen by forcing it. It is spontaneous when there is enough safety and when the client's attention is balanced between awareness of the present, positive reality and the past hurt. An awareness of the truth that the present moment is good, and healing is happening, provides safety and counteracts the hurt like a medicine antidotes a poison. This awareness provides an all-important perspective that makes the session a healing experience, instead of just a replaying of the old hurt one more time.

For example, if someone is very afraid that no one likes them, and it seems to them that you, the listener, also don't like them, they will not be able to heal and release the feeling. It seems to be true in the present time reality. If the listener can assure the client that they genuinely do like them, the client will feel safe. The client needs to see around their feelings, and have a little distance from them. Knowing the difference between how things feel and how they really are makes it is safe to release them. Feelings are not facts, they are temporary waves of experience.

19

The listener provides most of the reminders about the goodness and safety of the present moment. It is up to them to provide the balance.

Body Centered Techniques

There are a few body-centered ways of accessing emotion and encouraging catharsis.

Breathe! Distress around breathing is chronic, because holding your breath is one of the most effective ways to control discharge. Most people learn this early, and usually breathe with only about 20% of their lung capacity. Often simply attempting to breathe deeply in session will bring up incredible distress for discharge. Singing requires deep breaths, so often people will find they are pushing up against a deep control, and feel uncomfortable when singing.

Practice: Breathing
Try breathing shallow, then deeply and see what feeling arise when you do it for a few minutes. Then take slow deep breaths for about ten minutes.

All that is needed is to breathe a little more and a little deeper than usual, and to sustain that. Within a few minutes, emotions and body memories will spontaneously arise.

This is harder than it sounds- the habitual shallow breathing patterns take over quickly. The counselor must remind you to stay with the direction. It takes a lot of reminders to help someone keep breathing deeper than usual. You can keep breathing while releasing- or go back to breathing when the emotion slackens.

Sounds are really powerful in helping release. If their sounds seem choked or tense, encourage them to open up and relax their throat to avoid hurting it. We will explore using sounds in Chapter 6.

Physical action and movement is one of the most effective ways of getting into feelings. This might include hitting pillows, pillow fighting, pushing, wrestling, playing, stretching, pulling, squeezing, shaking and spontaneous movement.

Chapter 3:
Our Deepest Needs and Our Society

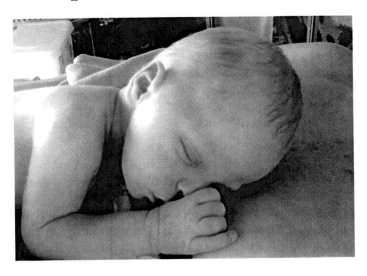

The Experience of Birth and Infancy

Imagine an idealized place where there is no need to do anything, because all your needs are met with no effort. You are completely united with an ever-present source of energy and love, feeling no separation of self and other. Surrounded and cushioned by a warm liquid of the perfect temperature, feeling safe, not needing to eat, to breathe, or to make any effort at all.

It is the proverbial Garden of Eden, a place of innocence and total relaxation. There is no struggle. Inside the womb, we feel our mother's every emotion and movement. Indeed, this is the time when we have the most closeness and intimacy with any other human being, and this translated as a feeling of closeness with the Creator.

Many do not experience the purity of this place, because their mothers may be distressed or unhealthy or drug addicted. However for most humans, the womb environment is the place that we remember vaguely, deep in our subconscious, as heaven. It is the original home.

The infant experiences the human mother as the Divine Mother, the source of all life and comfort. We are one with Her. Later experiences of sexuality are often colored by the longing to regain this lost feeling of oneness. We long for the feeling of unity.

As we grow, we become more cramped in our womb nest, and eventually the moment comes to emerge from the mother. Then huge forces begin to push and squeeze and move us outward. This is our first spiritual initiation, and it is also a strong initiation for the mother. We work together with our mother to make the change where our bodies separate.

We feel the cool air, and hear louder sounds, and feel the first touches directly on our skin. Then we take our first breaths, the blood stops pumping through the connecting cord, and our life on the outside begins. From then on, we must eat, and breathe, and communicate our needs to the others, who will hopefully be responsive, caring and gentle.

This entire process of birth, including all the emotions, physical sensations and events, becomes the foundational imprint on which our lives are based. It is the moment that gives us our first impression of what this world will be like, how much love there is, how hard or painful it might be, and who will be available for us to depend on. How our birth goes, and how we are handled immediately after it, has huge effects on our later lives. This has been thoroughly explored in the breath work therapy called Rebirthing, as taught by Leonard Orr and Sondra Ray.

A natural birth from a loving healthy mother is an experience of emerging from a total union with her body to a just slightly more separate state, where she is always still close and in skin contact all the time. As the baby grows older, this separation naturally grows stronger and it eventually becomes a self-supporting adult. In the tribal situations we used to live in, the child could explore leaving the mother's side when it felt ready.

Severe separation anxiety is not a requirement for a human incarnation. Yet even for those who have the most positive, gentle birth experiences, it is often felt as a deep loss and a primal wound of separation from the Creator. We feel ourselves as separate souls, encased in a separate body. Although our sense of self, our ego, takes years to develop, this is the beginning of the journey where we move through life as an individual entity. The free ride is over, and we need to increasingly take charge of caring for our own needs. Being cast from the Garden is a universal metaphor for our shared experience.

Effects of Modern Birthing Practices

The state of our society, and our emotional distress caused by centuries of unnatural lifestyles creates many blocks and painful experiences in the birthing process. The common practice of giving anesthesia to birthing mothers often results in infants being born with some numbness in their own bodies, which is disorienting and also causes physical stress and difficulty breathing. Sometimes it can affect the infant's heart and cause it to labor. It also makes an emotional and psychic disconnection with the mother at a time when bonding is most needed. Also many people experienced induced births, forceps births and cesareans, all of which create their own difficult emotional imprints. Often the father is not present, nor other caring family members, but only clinically detached doctors and nurses.

Many of us were taken from our mothers at birth, roughly handled, wrapped in fabric instead of having skin contact, and put in separate beds or rooms, exposed to bright lights, loud sounds, cold air, harsh chemicals and other stresses. Boys are routinely circumcised soon after birth, a brutal process that leaves many emotional scars and trust issues.

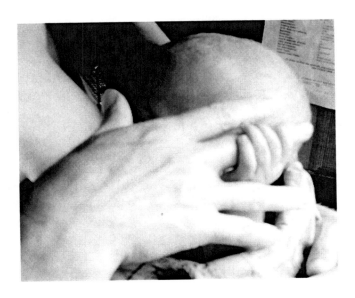

Many of us were not breast fed at all, and were fed and held only on schedule, with milk that was not ideally made for our bodies as our mother's milk is. Processed, cooked, dehydrated cow's milk formulas can create painful gastric problems for babies. Many of us were put apart from the mother to sleep, in separate beds and rooms. This is confusing and painful for an infant, because in that very young and vulnerable state, they crave the constant presence of the mother.

These practices are common in the Western world, and have resulted in many people with deep psychological and emotional imprints of being abused, unwanted and uncared for. It often leaves an imprint of abandonment, deep shock, physical pain and separation, and we are left with relying on objects such as blankets, food and pacifiers to meet very primal needs for mothering and human contact.

Our Natural Needs

We are genetically programmed to expect certain experiences after we are born. Infants expect and need total connection and physical contact with the mother directly after birth and for many months afterward. This is a deep and normal need on all levels, from the pure physical level of warmth and safety to the spiritual sense of continuing the total interconnectedness that was experienced in the womb. In many cultures, this is understood. In Bali, the babies are kept in arms until they are one year old.

We expect that adults will enjoy being close with us, and our mother will be pleased to nurse us and keep us near. Our DNA prepares us for the warm constant presence of many others, and perfectly designed breast milk with all the nutrients in the right proportions. We need to use our voice to express what we are really feeling, we need to be tended and cleaned, to be safe and sleep, and we need lots of love and attention.

In our ancient history of evolving in tribes, this situation was not hard to achieve. We grew up surrounded by brothers and sisters, cousins, aunts and uncles and grandparents, and had close connections with other families. There was always someone who wanted to hold the baby, and always others to play with. In many tribal cultures all the children and the parents share one sleeping space, with the youngest child having the place closest to the mother.

Our very recent evolution into a Western nuclear family lifestyle has created situations where one or two adults live alone with their children, and are expected to provide all of the child's need for

24

attention, stimulation, survival and love. As most parents in this situation have found out, this is an incredibly difficult, and exhausting task. Children want and need many people to draw from as teachers and nurturers, and playmates.

The arrangement of living in small separate houses in small families has created a great deal of stress and isolation, resulting in situations where parents are forced to choose between meeting their own needs or those of their children. Young people need far more stimulation and interaction that just one or two adults can provide. One estimate is that three to six adults per young person would be comfortably adequate to fill the needs of one child. Often the children outnumber the adults, and so the situation is very difficult. Child learn that they just have to live with not having enough.

On a daily basis, most children experience boredom, isolation, rejection and a sense of being too needy, being a pest, etc. Sometimes they are physically abused for expressing their natural needs, or just because the adults are unhappy. None of this is because the child has too many needs. Needs for attention, love and stimulation are natural and beautiful. Children never have too many needs. They just have more needs than the adults around can fulfill.

Feeling early needs in sessions is at first difficult for most people, since we have usually been shamed and even abused for having needs, and told what we need is too much. This arises from our very unhealthy culture, which isolates parents and places unrealistic expectations on them to be the sole provider of a child's needs. The idea that children should get "tough" early and get used to the "hard realities of life" is untrue and based on a hard view of life. If they get the love and attention they really need early in life, they will have an inner strength that will carry them well through later pain. The first seven years are especially important and provide the foundation of a person's personality structure.

After a time of experiencing the lack of needs being met, children develop what can be called "frozen needs" (a term from Re-evaluation Co-counseling). Someone with frozen needs seems to be unable to be satisfied not matter how much they are given. Nothing ever seems to be enough.

Old Frozen Needs VS Current Needs

People of any age do have real, current needs that can be filled, and the levels of those needs change according to age and life situation. We all have the need to love, need to be loved and respected, need for touch, sleep, food, emotional release, satisfying work, exercise, a healthy environment, and creative expression. Non-violent Communication is a modality that focuses a lot on identifying our needs, respecting them and expressing them clearly.

Frozen needs are created when there is an unfilled real need. They happen when real current needs are not met at the right time, and the resulting hurt was not expressed, understood or processed. Then the needy feeling gets frozen into place into rigid and compulsive actions. It becomes a recording of the old need which plays endlessly when one is reminded of anything similar to the old situation.

These are usually created in early childhood, when we were dependent, had many physical & emotional needs. For example, a baby needs to suck and nurse a lot, and if this real oral need is not filled, then the frozen needs can develop into later desires to smoke, chew gum, or eat to much.

We can identify a frozen need whenever there is a wanting for something that is never satisfied. It feels like there is never enough love, food, attention, etc, even if you are really getting a lot of these

26

things. We may be completely full after a big meal, and still feel like we want to eat more.

The desperate feeling of wanting may sometimes be covered by a feeling of aversion, or distaste, as a defense against feeling the need underlying. For example, anorexia is where the person has an obsession around food, but they cannot allow themselves to take much of it in. Someone may become convinced that sex is evil, because of their fear of the intense power of the longing.

Jealousy is a great example where we see frozen needs reveal themselves. When you find yourself wanting all your partner's attention all the time, this is a result of not getting enough attention when a child. This kind of need for constant attention is normal feeling when you are very young, but the feeling gets stuck there.

Frozen needs can't be filled, they can only be felt and released. We must face the reality that we can never be in that old situation again. We will not be two years old again, and the chance for that need to be truly filled has been lost. Now we can only feel how it felt not to have the need met, and grieve for that lost opportunity. This grieving process is very important, and if there has not been time to release the pain, it stays stuck and acts as a block to real satisfaction in the moment.

Many adult relationships involved in trying to get frozen needs filled by the present partner. Trying to fill a frozen need is exhausting, and it can't be done, and trying to do so for another person leaves you a drained feeling.

Can you think of examples in your own life? When have you tried to satisfy someone, who can never be satisfied? Do you have the sense that no one has ever truly satisfied you?

We have very different needs as a adult than we did as a child. Children rely on adults for their survival and have real and deep needs to stimulation, learning and interaction to feed their growing brain and body. Adults can normally take care of their own survival, and are not growing and learning at the incredible rate of a child. When you allow yourself to feel the childlike, needy feelings and release them, you will be able to get to a much more appropriate and realistic level of what you really need now.

Filling a real, current time need can be done, and it is satisfying and enjoyable. If we did not have old programmed needs obscuring our experience, we would be able to eat a meal of a normal amount, and feel satisfied. We would be able to easily sleep a good night's sleep, and

27

wake up refreshed. We would have a time of cuddling and closeness, and feel satisfied, and then be ready to move on to something else, without the nagging feeling that it was not quite enough. As we release the old imprint of early needs, these experiences become much more possible in our present time life.

Working with Frozen Needs

When we are working with our inner child selves, we are almost certainly working with frozen old needs. It is helpful to know some information about how to work with them. Our goal is to think clearly, and respond freshly and appropriately to each new situation. Frozen needs are powerful recordings pulling from the reptilian brain, which can easily fog our rational thinking.

It can get complicated identifying what is a frozen need, because we have ongoing present time needs, like for touching and love, AND layers of frozen needs around it. How can we tell the difference? How do we know if that desire for time with are partner is coming from our inner child's old needs, or our actual present time need as an adult? Do we really need that extra slice of pizza?

"Feelings" is a confusing word, because it is used to mean emotion, physical sensation and intuitive knowing. We can separate feelings into natural, inherent feelings in humans, such as zestful enjoyment of living, and distressed emotions which come from hurtful events, like sorrow, self hate, anger, etc.

Emotions are not reliable guides for action. One day you may feel like killing someone, the next you've cooled off. If you act on the distressed emotion, without thinking clearly about the long term effects of your actions, usually it doesn't have a helpful result.

Sometimes it's hard to tell which are distressed feelings. Some distressed feelings can be described as feeling good, or even delightful by people in the grips of recordings. For example, smoking, taking a drink, taking revenge, and addictive romantic pulls can all be defended as feeling "good" in the moment. However the long term effects are destructive.

An addiction is when we substitute a behavior or substance for what we really need, and this keeps the feelings down about how we aren't getting what we want and need. Almost like we fool ourselves into accepting a cheap substitute because "it's better than nothing". Addictions are survival strategies from situations where we needed some kind of comfort, or at least a way to numb the pain.

When counseling on additions or frozen needs, let yourself feel how much you want it, but don't act on the desire. Go to earliest memory of that feeling, and stay there.

Feel your feelings and act on your clear thinking. Act on what you know is right, not on fleeting emotions. Good feelings can be enjoyed, and bad feelings can be released. If your feelings go along with your thinking, then great. If not, then acting on your inner clarity will bring up the feelings for discharge.

For example, if someone has been acting in a way that hurts you, such as lying about you to others, you may know that the right thing to do is to confront them and ask them about it. However, you may have feelings of fear or anger that urge you to either avoid the situation, or try to hurt the person back. Releasing those feelings in a session will make it easier to act with calm clarity in the moment.

What Parents Need

Humans were created as creatures that live in groups, and everyone needs lots of friends and allies. Especially parents, who are being depended on by young ones for all their needs. Parents are not supported much in this huge job by the society in the United States. In our culture there is little financial support for raising children, or taking parenting sabbaticals from work, or subsidies for childcare. Parents are often given the message that they must do it all themselves, and do it perfectly. Many parents attempt more than they are able to do, and feel guilty for failing in the impossible task they believe they must do alone.

Every parent does their very best, given the amount of pain they carry from their own past, and obstacles they face externally. Every parent would love to see their child do well, and to feel that their child was happy. Often these feelings of love are buried under a mountain of pain, which causes the parent to be self-absorbed, without much to offer the child.

It is very important to reach out past the isolation and false pride and get help. We are trained to isolate into nuclear families, and not seek out the allies and resources we need to raise healthy children. It takes many adults and other children to meet the ongoing needs of a young person in a relaxed way.

Food, Love and Touch

The most important needs of an infant, beside basic safety, are food, love, and touch. As we create a therapeutic space for working with out deepest infantile imprints, we are working directly with these areas.

Think for a minute about what food is. What is it for, on a physical level? A brainstorm will bring up words like: strengthening, nurturing, life giving, healing, satisfying, sustaining.

Now think about what love is. How do you feel when you are loved? You may come up with words like: warm, appreciated, wanted, full, satisfied, healed, strengthened.

Practice: Food and Love

Write or discuss this: When were you given food instead of love? When you were fed, what were the adults feeling? Were they happy to feed you? Did you get enough food? Enough love?

In the beginning of our lives, food and love are almost the same. Food is one physical expression of love. It usually comes from our mother. We come into the world expecting a lot of touching, sucking, and food that is just right for our bodies, digestible and nourishing, on demand. What else does a baby get while nursing, besides nutrition? Attention, warmth, safety, skin contact, loving, closeness.

All of these are real, present needs. For infants, nursing is an affirmation of our goodness, that we are worthwhile, valuable. We naturally expect to be loved, cared for and cherished. If we are not experiencing this, it hurts and we become confused about the world and our own value.

As adults, the way we feed ourselves is an expression of how much we love and value ourselves, and often reflects our early hurts about how well we were nourished when very young.

When something is missing from the expected unconditional love and perfect nourishment, this creates distress. If the food is given with impatience, or no attention or cuddling, or the food is hard to digest (cow's milk is generally hard, especially if it is cooked), we experience hurt. It creates frozen needs, which are exact recordings of the feelings of the real needs not being filled.

What distress gets created? Try thinking about how you feel when you have been expecting love and attention and you don't get it: sad, rejected, worthless, lonely, or abandoned. Children tend to turn these feelings inward, and believe there is something wrong with them, rather than believe that the parents are acting wrongly.

30

The root of every emotional pattern is some variation of the feeling "I am bad". This feeling of self-invalidation is also underneath food problems. There is usually a huge amount of shame, guilt and embarrassment around food. We become more rational, healthy and loving the more we do our emotional healing and come to see that we are basically good, and always have been.

Distress around food is often similar to distress around sex and touch, since early eating experiences are also times of getting love and touching. Babies need to be held almost constantly, for stimulation and safety (seen in tribal cultures where the babies are carried). It is a huge need. If they only get held while being fed, they will REALLY want that feeding time, and seek to prolong it. If, instead of aware attention while the are crying, they get food shoved at them, the food becomes part of habit of controlling emotions.

In many families it is not OK for us to touch, cuddle and share feelings with our family members while growing up, and one of the few outlets for expressing love is food. We make special treats for each other, giving it as a reward, and giving it as a substitute for comfort when upset. It becomes one small channel attempting to satisfy a lot of huge emotional needs. It becomes much more emotionally significant than it would be rationally.

31

In this culture, the distress around food is very deep, and most of us begin being exposed it as soon as we are born. It sticks to everything, connecting to other issues like powerlessness, adultism and sexism. Like sex, this culture seems obsessed with food. It is very hard for most of us to think clearly about food until we have worked thoroughly on the topic.

Practice: Breastfeeding History

In pairs, do a short listening session trade with someone, or write in your journal. What happened in your life around breastfeeding? How did your mother feel about it? How did you feel? How and when were you weaned, and how did that feel?

Chapter 11.
The Heartbeat Nurturing Process

This is a brief introduction to the overall process of Heartbeat Nurturing, and ways you might use it. The rest of the book gives details on all the specific aspects of the process.

Sessions can be sweet and light, given for just a few minutes of close contact, or they can be hours long and involve some very deep catharsis. They can be done clothed, partially clothed, or nude. They can be extremely intimate or just a gentle friendly contact. It all depends on the needs and energy of the two people participating in the moment.

The basic form can be used between friends, parents and children, clients and therapists, or to comfort someone who is ill or injured. It is very flexible in its applications.

For the Giver

Please read through the entire book before you do a session for someone, so that you have a more clear idea about what feelings may arise for them, and for you. This process leads us in to very deep and sensitive emotional territory, so be sure you are prepared.

33

Only give a session when you are in a good mood, well rested and feeling clear. Be willing to take guidance from the receiver so you can most accurately give them what they are wanting. During the giving, concentrate completely on them, and generating a feeling of loving kindness and appreciation.

Giving a session is a moment where you are invited to step out of your usual self and become a channel or embodiment of your deeper self. Open yourself to the Divine, however you conceive of it. Let a large force of love come through you. Your intention to do this will greatly enhance the healing that happens.

Also take care of yourself, and if they want something you can't feel comfortable doing, it is your right to say no, and propose a substitute that would feel better to you. If you find yourself unable to give loving attention and stay present for them, it is better to end the session gently and excuse yourself, and explain that you want to take care of your own needs. Come back to it another time.

For the Receiver

Set it up so you can get comfortable in a safe and quiet place. You might want a pillow or other object to hold on to. It's a time to nurture yourself and allow any emotions that arise to flow freely, as this is a big part of the healing process. Let yourself completely relax. Allow time afterward to integrate the experience.

Keep in mind that the giver has agreed to nurture you for the time during the session, and has not automatically signed up for a longer contract. What happens during the session does not mean anything about what will happen afterward.

The giver is attempting to get out of the way and channel Divine love and healing to you, which does not mean they will be able or willing to do it when they are back in their daily activities. It is a special ritual and moment for healing, set apart from our normal daily life and personalities. Enjoy it for what it is.

You may feel emotionally vulnerable or physically tired afterward for a day or two, if the session moves some deep emotions. You may feel unreasonable emotions afterward, either positive or negative, toward your giver. Be prepared to take responsibility for your own experience as an individual. Know that you are in charge of your session and if the giver is doing something that does not work, it is up to you to let them know. If you need to ask for a correction, do it in a

34

positive way, by asking for what you want, rather than telling them what they are doing wrong.

Short & Simple Heartbeat Sessions

It is wonderful to spend a few moments being close. Even five minutes, without any preamble or ritual around it, can be very healing.

Begin by agreeing on how long you will do the cradling. Get comfortable either sitting or laying down, and cradle the receiver's head near the giver's heart (ideally skin to skin, but that is not necessary), softly stroking the face and shoulders. You may want to try singing, humming or speaking words that the receiver may have wished to hear from their own mother or father. Try also speaking in "gibberish" or with meaningless words, since infants have no word recognition. Or just put on soothing music and hold silence.

The session may be done clothed or not. If they want to include oral stimulation, use a thumb or other nipple substitute, or just enjoy being held or cradled.

Give the receiver a minute warning before the session is to end. Help them sit up, look around the room and come back to normal consciousness. If you like, then trade places, and have them hold you for a while.

Practice: Short Cradling Session

Find a friend or lover and exchange a short cradling session. Do another one with someone of the other gender, so you get the feeling of being both fathered and mothered. Discuss it with them afterward.

Giving a Full Session

Decide how long you have to do a session. One hour is a good amount of time, yet 1 and 1/2 hours or 2 will give more completion. The initial interview can take 30 minutes or an hour by itself, so be sure to pace the session. Allow at least 5 to 20 minutes at the end to transition and finish.

Preparing For the Session

Initial Interview

Start by discussing these questions, or write the answers:

What is their birth history? Where, how, what happened?

How was their relationship with their mother or father? (Depending on what gender the therapist is, choose one parent role for the session).

What was their breastfeeding experience, and nighttime sleep experience?

How did this affect them?

What would they have loved to get more of from their mother/father?

Mama/Papa Message Design:

Ask what they most wanted to hear from their mother/father, write it down.

Ask how they would most like to be touched by their parent.

Setting intent for this session: Ask them what their intent is.

Creating a Sacred Context

We can create a sacred space in many ways. It can be very elaborate or very simple, depending on your own style and needs. If you are not so interested in the spiritual aspect, you might make it as simple as just breathing together a few times, and looking in each other's eyes for a few minutes.

Prepare the Room

Light candles, put on soft music, drape fabrics around, light incense, put crystals around the room, and arrange lots of pillows. You may want some snuggly blankets around. Turn off the phone and make sure you will not be interrupted by anyone. Turn down the lights or pull the shades.

Prepare Yourself as a Giver

Practice meditation and clearing your energy before the session, and invoking your inner sources of energy. Put on special clothes or jewelry if you like, or a loose robe you plan to take off. Bathe beforehand if needed.

36

(See Chapter 8. Getting Your Energy Clear)

Aspects of Creating Sacred Space

Usually rituals contain these elements in some form. Choose which ones you like to include. Or skip them if you are not so inclined.

(See Chapter 9. Invoking the Divine).

Purification & Blessing

This might be anointing with oils or water, smudging, brushing the energy body, etc. This just reminds us to let go of whatever we don't need right now, and helps us come into the present moment.

Grounding

Sitting together in meditation, connecting to the earth energy, deep slow breathing, eye contact.

Making the Container

Visualize a circle of light or state out loud that this is a safe space for opening and healing. Call the energies of the four directions of east, south, west and north, or however you like to create awareness of the sacred.

Invocations: Calling on Higher Energies

Do an invocation internally, and also out loud as desired, of Divine energy. Invoke the energy of the Divine Mother Goddess, or the Divine Father.

The process can be done without the spiritual context, but we have found that it adds greatly to the effectiveness of the sessions, and helps reduce transference problems.

You might call in the presence of your teachers and guides, or of archetypes of the God or Goddess that you relate to, or power animals, angels, etc.

Then do the main work of the healing session, as outlined below.

The Heartbeat Nurturing Therapy Processes

The Basic Process

The basic process can be use in a short and simple session with anyone. It can be spontaneous, like a time when someone is very upset or ill and needs comfort. It works well, of course, with actual children.

The basic process is the same as used in the sort sessions, and involves cradling the head near the heart (ideally skin to skin), so the heartbeat can be heard, softly stroking the face and shoulders, while singing or speaking words that the receivers may have wished to hear from their own mother or father. The basic practice may be done clothed or not, using a thumb or other nipple substitute, or just cradling.

Cradling:

Invite them to put their head on your heart, OR do this after the regression. Find the most comfortable position.

(See Chapter 7 for photos of suggested positions).

Regression/ Hypnotic induction:

With the client lying on your chest or near you, begin with a basic guided relaxation, with deep breathing, for at least 5 minutes. (Chapter 6. Nurturing and Healing With The Voice)

Then invite them to go back in time to when they were a child, and ask permission to speak to them as though they are a child now.
(See Chapter 12: Regression to the Inner Child, and Chapter 5. Inner Child Work)

As appropriate:

Encourage the client to make baby sounds, thumb sucking

Speak in gibberish or other languages

Humming, toning or singing lullabies

(See Chapter 6)

Optional Meditation: Meeting the God/dess

Guide them in imagining that they are being held by the Mother goddess or Father God, totally adored by Her/Him. Speak as though the Divine voice is coming through you.

(See Chapter 12: Meeting the Mother Goddess Meditation)

Alternatively, you can guide them to imagine that you are the more aware representative of their mother or father. You can role play the Good Parent, or Aware Parent.

Advanced Process: Suckling

For lovers and others who might want to explore deeper territory, the advanced form is powerful. This process includes the receiver nuzzling and touching the breasts, as a baby would, and the offering of a breast for suckling. We have found that the actual shape and texture of a real breast is the best for effectively changing the deepest patterning. The somatic re-patterning of the brain is very powerful, especially if the receiver is identified with their inner child self at the moment of the suckling. (See Chapter 10. Reclaiming our Breasts)

Finishing the session

The components of this finishing step might be:

Bringing the infant back through time, growing up with the new imprints

Bringing the Divine/Good Parent back with them more fully

Remembering all that has happened in the session and integrating this into the adult persona

Thanking and cherishing the infant self

Resting time for integration and spooning, with the giver lying next to them hugging them from behind.

Drifting to sleep, letting go, laying them down

(Chapter 12. Coming Back Home Meditation)

Waking up, Coming Back to Normal

Guide them in coming back to a more normal waking state, feeling refreshed and alert, remembering everything they experienced. Taking breaths wiggling fingers and toes, lifting your arms and legs up and down a little. When they feel ready, move a little more and then open the eyes slowly. Stretch, roll on one side and get up, look around the room. Ask them questions about the present moment, such as what they see in the room.

After the Session

Discussion and integration

How do they feel now? Anything they want to share?

Action steps

Ask them how can they include more self-nurturing in their lives? Help them brainstorm. This helps them create more of what they need outside of sessions, and to come back into their adults selves.

Release the Sacred Space

Give thanks to the energies you called on, release of energies, send the blessings out to share with others

Imagine opening and dissolving the circle you created for healing work.

Clearing Afterward

Do some aura combing, grounding, visualizing light, hand sweeps, or just washing your hands

Be sure to clear your own energy and separate out from the client so you do not carry away the energy they let go of in their session.

(Chapter 8. Getting Your Energy Clear)

Confidentiality

Avoid bringing up whatever happened later, outside of session. Don't discuss it or refer to it with the client without carefully asking permission and making very sure it is a good time. Do not discuss it with anyone else. Respect their privacy.

Trading Sessions

If you want to exchange a session, you can do it after a short break, or you can do it at a later time after the person has had time to integrate. Decide what feels best in the moment.

The next chapters will give you the background to understand the processes we are doing, and why they are effective.

It is especially important to read them if you are not already a trained therapist or co-counselor.

Chapter 5.
Inner Child Work

Giving Voice to The Inner Parts

Emotionally, we are made up of many different feelings, patterns and habits, which can be looked at as separate aspects of our personality. They can be called sub-personalities or personas, or just patterns. Each of these inner voices has an important message for the whole being, and a role to play.

We can see this reflected in our physical body, where there are many different cells, which each have a small separate life force, which cooperate and group into larger organs, each of which has a separate function and life force. The key to health is to have each of these separate parts cooperating with all the others for a common good. Cancer cells are an example of a cell that has forgotten its connection to the whole, and it multiplies wildly, with no awareness of the health of the host organism, ultimately destroying it unless stopped. Chronic disease is a physical expression of a disconnected inner shadow self.

Often we are trained to ignore or discount some of our inner voices or feelings, because they are not socially acceptable in some way. We come to feel bad and guilty about having certain feelings and thoughts, and we hide them even from ourselves, so the parts of us that hold those feelings effectively become cut off from communication with the whole.

Sometimes a very hurtful event happens that we do not have the strength to face at that time, so it gets stored or buried in a hidden sub-personality. These lost parts of ourselves are areas that we avoid because they feel so uncomfortable to remember, but they are the areas that need healing and attention the most. They hold important lessons and strengths.

Seeking them out in counseling sessions and inviting them to come forward into the conscious mind lets us get to know them and therefore integrate them back into ourselves. This also robs them of any power they may have to surprise us and pop up unexpectedly, at awkward moments. Being able to act our various inner voices gives us flexibility and freedom in our definition of who we are. If we are limited to only a few very narrow personality traits, we can become rigid and dogmatic, with very strong beliefs about what is the right and wrong way to be.

Many therapies have integrated these ideas, including RC, voice dialogue work, Process work and inner child work. Theater requires people to discover and identify with many inner personas, so actors may find this easy. Here are some suggestions for beginning to work in this way.

Three Selves: Adult, Child and Higher Self

In many indigenous traditions, three primary inner selves are worked with. The adult self is our conscious waking self, the ego definition we usually identify with. If someone asks you "Who are you?" you will answer with the voice of the adult self.

This is the self who thinks rationally and logically, who keeps life going by working and tending to what needs to be done. The adult is the parent and caregiver, and usually dominates a person's awareness. It keeps things under control, and does what is needed to protect itself. It is also the barrier that keeps us feeling separate from other life forms. The stronger the adult ego is, the more there is a sense of separate selfhood. Ideally we want a strong yet flexible adult, with healthy boundaries but able to relax when needed. The adult self is a good servant, but not a good master, in terms of guiding a life.

The Higher Self or Deeper Self is the aspect of the soul that is spiritual and in touch with energies beyond the physical limitations of matter. It is the self that gives us guidance, creative inspiration, and a

42

sense of our deep connectedness with all that is. We tune in to the deeper self when we meditation or go into trance states. It is the source of love and energy and power.

The Child Self or Younger Self is the emotional, gut level, intuitive, animal self. Younger Self holds the ancient knowledge of how to be a healthy animal in a body, how to play, how to feel, how to have pleasure, and how to let emotions flow through. This self is wild and free, and follows what feels good. It has been greatly suppressed through our Western culture, because people who are really free and fully feeling are very hard to control.

Younger Self is the gateway to the Divine, and many traditions say that a person cannot know Spirit directly without going through the inner magical child. This is what Jesus was saying when he said: "Those who seek the kingdom of Heaven must come as a little child". The inner child is the key to our happiness and joy in life. Spending time freeing and healing our inner children is a powerful way to finding inner peace.

The goal for this therapy is to encourage all the parts to become friends, to love each other and accept each part's existence. A typical process would be a hurt inner child persona being loved and accepted by the parental adult persona. Or the adult might be guided by the child.

Letting these voices speak is an altered state of consciousness, a little like being in a dream state.

Identify the Inner Self and Get Permission

In this therapy we work with the inner child. You can also use this process for any inner persona. Begin by identifying an inner child of a certain age. Always talk directly to the inner part as though it was a separate person. This is a very effective aspect of the technique. Think of talking "past" the conscious self, ignoring it for a moment.

Always be respectful of all the parts you are speaking with, including those acting as oppressors. If the voices are full of hateful or shameful or weak feelings, it is because they have been hurt and discounted. Remember that each part is important and needs to be fully honest and listened to with respect. Every part is trying to meet to real need inside the whole.

Ask if the dominant conscious ego personality, (who the person usually is identified with being) will allow you to talk to the inner child self. This is important because the conscious self often will interrupt with critical thoughts or act as interpreter for the sub-personality.

43

Remember, the reason this persona needs help to talk is that the conscious self is uncomfortable with its feelings and opinions.

It is important to get the conscious self to be quiet for a while and allow the lost parts to come forward. This takes courage and trust. But this process itself helps the conscious self to see that the "bad" feelings are only a small part of the whole self, and that makes it safer for people to explore them. Say things like "Can you let this other part take over for a while, so we can find out what it is?"

Ask the inner persona that you are trying to reach if it will speak with you. This is important, as sometimes the inner self is very shy and scared, or hostile and rebellious. If it won't, perhaps another inner self will speak, or it will use movement or non-verbal sounds. Usually they are glad to be getting any attention. To access and very young self, who is preverbal, you will need to act like a child does, such as making infant sounds and movements.

Talking to the Persona/Inner Child

In general, you want to give the inner child a chance to tell its own opinion and feelings. Address it by its name. "Hello, little _____, I would like to find out about who you are." Ask it things like "tell me how you feel" and "what is it you want most?" Encourage it to release emotions and express itself. Give lots of appreciation ("you are perfect just as you are") and validations ("of course you feel that way"), to show that you understand its point of view. Reassure it that this is a safe time to talk, and that you are really interested in what it has to say, if it needs those counteractions. In short, counsel it as you would anyone.

Encourage the person to talk directly from that part, such as "I am really jealous" and not "this part is really jealous." This will make it much more real and immediate.

Practice: Speak With the Inner Child

Either with a partner or in writing by yourself, go inside and invite an inner child to speak with you. Let the child self use your voice, and do not censor what comes out, even if it makes no sense. Thank and appreciate the child afterward.

Finishing the Dialogue

Ask if this voice has any final things to say to the conscious self. When it seems time to stop, thank that inner part for sharing, and move back to the original position, and encourage the person to come back fully to their normal conscious self

What Happens to Young People

In exploring our own inner child, it is helpful to think about how children are treated. What are children naturally like? Think for a minute about what children are like before they are programmed and trained by the parents and society.

Young people are in a position of dependence and lack of experience, and so are especially vulnerable to being hurt by the distresses of the adults around them. But unless they are made to feel powerless, they are not. They have powerful voices and strong ideas about what they need and want, from the time they are born. They are very intelligent, and can figure things out well, given the time and information and support they need.

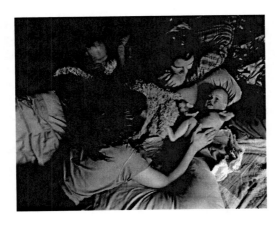

Our culture tends to view children as needing to be molded, disciplined and taught how to do things right. This is distress stemming from when the adult's own process of learning was interfered with as a child. People have a deep inherent longing to learn about the world, and will do so eagerly, in their own way, in their own time, if allowed to. Young people often see things more clearly than adults, since they do not usually have as many layers of distress over their thinking. They will often point out clearly any irrational distress patterns in the adults around them. They often are more in touch with their inner spirituality, psychic awareness and communication with animals, plants and energy beings. They are often more openly loving, joyous and playful than adults. In truth, children are important spiritual teachers, each with special gifts for the adults around them.

The oppression of young people is systematically enforced by our society, economics, and traditions in the culture. Teachers and childcare workers are underpaid and disrespected. The message of young people's oppression is "the younger you are, the less important you are." It is one of disrespect and lack of importance, wherein the young person is not listened to or consulted about decisions relating to their lives. They are patronized and talked down to as cute but unimportant people.

Everyone grows up looking forward to a later time when they will be older and hopefully be treated with more respect. This oppression is the only one that you can expect to grow out of. It is the only one where you will someday change roles and be the adult who gets to make the decisions and have respect. Others, like sexism and racism, will be present your entire life.

This oppression is also the basis of all others, since the messages of worthlessness, insignificance, helplessness, and abandonment get internalized, and leave the person very vulnerable to later distress imprints from sexism, racism, religious oppression, etc.

Practice: Childhood Memories

Can you think of things you were told by adults as a young person, or ways you were treated, that were disrespectful and oppressive? How were you treated by older children? Have a short counseling session on this, or write it down.

Practice: Meeting the Younger Self

Begin with a basic guided relaxation, with deep breathing, for at least 5 minutes. Have someone read the Guided Regression To The Inner Child in Chapter 12 to you slowly, or record it so you listen as you do the regression

Emotional Release on Physical Hurts

In working with early infant memories and imprints, another thing that often arises is being hurt physically. This might have happened from another person hurting us, or just from the normal process of growing up. Often the birth process is physically uncomfortable. Chronic tension in the body is always related to emotions.

Emotional release about a physical hurt seems to greatly improve the healing process. Most people have strong emotions about being hurt physically, and putting aware attention directly on the emotions releases a lot of tension. People who have used this process often experience faster physical healing of an acute injury, and relief from long term symptoms. Releasing the emotions around a hurt seems to free up the body's natural healing powers and increase immune system functioning.

The basic technique for working on physical hurts is to tell the story of what happened, repeatedly and in detail, and allow space for the emotions to come to the surface. Many people naturally want to tell the story anyway. The counselor needs to be attentive and interested and encouraging.

In Heartbeat Therapy, the story may not come out until after the emotions are experienced in the actual session, when the client has come back to their verbal adult persona. The counselor and even the client may not know what is going on until afterward, and that is fine.

Typical physical traumas that may arise are anesthesia or circumcision. Anesthesia leaves an imprint in the psyche of numbness, helplessness and being disassociated. If you suddenly find yourself falling asleep in a session, or having a heavy, dead, lazy sensation, these could be impressions from early actual experiences arise to be healed. Do your best to stay present with them, and to describe them to your counselor. Talk about how numb and dead you feel, and let yourself stretch and yawn.

Circumcision memories may bring feelings of abandonment, mistrust, terror and tension. If you can access these feelings and let yourself be held while you feel them, this is ideal and will have deep healing effects. Let yourself scream and shake and push with your arms and legs, while you are held. If a counselor can be present with you through this, the energy released will make profound changes in your energy level and ease in your body.

Working with Old Physical Hurts

For an old hurt, one that has already healed physically, always counsel on the **emotional hurts around the event.** This might be an operation, or a car accident, circumcision, birth trauma, or some other

47

event that you know was traumatic and you want to clear up. The physical hurt will naturally discharge once the emotions are dealt with.

Focusing too much on the details of the physical aspects could bring the hurt back, to be re-experienced on the physical level, if it is worked on directly (by describing how much it hurt, in exactly what way, etc.). People have reported old bruises and other symptoms re-appearing after counseling on a hurt. It is not always necessary to re-experience the physical pain on this level in order to release it. So focus on how it felt emotionally, when telling the story.

Sometimes strong pains emerge in sessions, because the body memory is releasing stored energy from the cells. If you do find a physical pain emerging during the session, just be interested in it and focus on what message it is bringing. Resisting it will increase the pain. Welcome it as a messenger, and get curious. Why should your head suddenly start to hurt at that moment? Often even intense pains will disappear immediately after the session is over.

Catharsis may come as physical (yawning, trembling) or emotional (tears, laughter, etc). This process will help pain and shock, and will make it heal faster. Many people have reported incredibly fast healing using this direction.

Making non-word sounds seems especially effective, (try yelling "OW!") and encouraging stretching, shaking and movement of any kind.

Resting Deeply

Resting is a great direction to use in your sessions, and is a natural part of Heartbeat Therapy, where you are cradled in someone's arms. Let yourself completely relax, with nothing to do, nothing to say. It helps to have the client lay down and close their eyes. The counselor can assure the client that they don't need the client to do anything to entertain them, they can just let go, etc.

Concentrate as a counselor on totally appreciating and loving the person while they do nothing. Calmly give loving messages, which the client is not required to repeat aloud, but they often need to hear. Keep speaking every few minutes, in a low voice, saying things like "It is safe to relax. You don't have to do anything to take care of me. Set everything aside for just a few minutes. Let the world go on without you."

This counteracts some very basic chronic feelings for many people, such as the feeling that it is not OK to just be, and that you have

48

to do something to be accepted. This is an especially effective direction for many men, whose engrained performance patterns may often interfere with discharge in sessions.

At first the client may have many feelings come up as they attempt to totally relax, and as always, encourage any catharsis. A good direction for many people is to have the counselor stand guard against the imagined threats of the patterns, ex: "I will keep watch now, so you can rest. I won't let anyone come near. I will take over all your responsibilities."

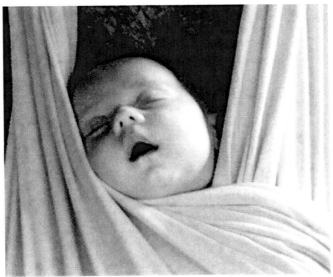

After a while, the client will be able to relax well enough to go to sleep during a session, and this is a very healing experience for many people, to sleep with attention. As a counselor, keep your attention on the client while they sleep. Think about what a precious and special person they are. You can keep giving them loving messages if you like, as these are absorbed very well by the subconscious while someone is sleeping. Admire them. And wake them slowly up when it is time for the session to be over.

Practice: Deep Resting

In pairs, have one person lay down and just completely rest for a while. Reassure them that you will stand guard, and there is nothing for them to do. If they have resistance or fears arise, encourage them to let you know. Then trade.

49

Chapter 6.
Nurturing and Healing with The Voice

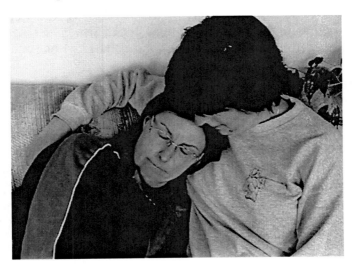

Hypnotic Induction and Regression

Relaxation is a skill that can be practiced, and has huge health benefits. One of the most important aspects of Heartbeat Nurturing is helping people to relax, let go, and soften out of their adult personas. We do this primarily through vocal tone, heartbeat sounds and touch. If the giver is relaxed, and the touch and voice is slow and gentle, this induces a deep hypnotic trance state.

Trance and Suggestibility

A trance state is when the body relaxes, and the brain waves slow down from the normal beta waves that characterize our waking state, and our adult self. Alpha states can be induced fairly easily and have been researched extensively for changing behavior patterns easily. Any time someone is daydreaming, visualizing, or meditating, these brain changes happen, and have healing effects on the whole body. Also music, rhythmic lights, singing, dancing, exercise, sexual excitement and pleasure states create a similar effect.

Listening to the heartbeat sound is one of the most powerful ways to calm and relax someone. Recordings of womb sounds and heartbeats, and even music with a heartbeat rhythm, has been used to calm infants, animals and severely injured people.

When someone is in an altered state, it seems that the capacity to change and re-record old patterns is really enhanced. It is as though the control of the adult self has let go, and the self is free to melt and shift and find more new patterns. We become much more suggestible. This has been studied extensively by the advertizing industry as a way to induce people to desire to buy things. It can also be used as a way to consciously re-program one's feelings and beliefs, get out of addictions, and resolve old pain.

We use this way to make changes involving our infancy and birth, by willingly going into a deep relaxation and trance, doing a regression where we imagine becoming young again, and replaying the story the way we wish it had been.

Giving a Guided Meditation

The most important thing for a therapist giving a meditation is to be relaxed inside. Staying in a peaceful, quiet inner space will communicate that energy to the client. Several practices are suggested in Chapter 8 for how to do this.

Vocal Stroking

Imagine that your voice is a way to caress another person. Using gentle, resonant vocal tones and speaking loving words can be thought of as vocal stroking. Think of petting them with your voice.

Use your vocal tone and pacing consciously. Your voice can be played like a musical instrument. When guiding a trace, your voice should be low and smooth, and speaking much more slowly than normal. Saying a few words and then pausing, and then saying another phrase, makes a rhythmic element to the words and helps with trance.

Whispering can be a nice addition as well, especially if you whisper right next to their ear. This creates an intimate feeling and is often done by parents while cradling infants.

Sensory Styles

People have different ways of learning, and ways that they perceive the world. Some people are stronger in their different senses. There are visual, emotional, tactile, and hearing oriented people. Education therapists who help children with learning challenges have studied this extensively. We want to keep this in mind as we are working with a client.

If someone is more visually oriented, we might make more comments that relate to sight, such as "See yourself getting younger and younger. How do you look when you are five years old?" For a more emotional or physically oriented person, you would use the word "feel" more often, such as "Feel yourself getting smaller....remember how it felt to have small arms and legs..." For hearing oriented people, we might ask them to remember the sound of their mother's voice, or the sounds of their old house. Ask your client what they are strongest in, and tailor your guided meditation to them.

Practice: Record Your Own Guided Relaxation

Take a moment and either write your own deep relaxation, or use the Guided Deep Relaxation Meditation in Chapter 12. You can design it to be just right for you.

Record it in your own voice, with some relaxing music in the background. Then lie down in a dark quiet place and practice letting your self become completely relaxed.

Positive Message Design

When we are in a session with someone acting as our surrogate parent, we want to help them nurture us as effectively as possible. So we spend time before the session designing affirmations and messages for them to say to us when we are in our altered state of relaxation.

The power of affirmations is well known and used throughout many therapies and spiritual manifestation practices.

An affirmation is a statement of what you would like to be true, stated in present time and in the affirmative. If you would like to believe that you are truly lovable, a statement like "I am not hated by others" would not be effective. Apparently the subconscious mind does not hear the "not" part very well. Also a statement like "I will be deeply loved by others" is not as powerful as "I am deeply loved by others".

When you are designing your Mama or Papa Messages, think of what infants would love to hear, if they could understand the meaning of the words. What did you crave to hear from your parent?

The therapist might also try channeling spontaneous messages from the Deeper Self. What would the Divine Mother feel about her precious child? What would She say?

53

Practice: Personal Message Design
Write down what you most wanted to hear from your mother. Make another list of what you wanted to hear from your father.

Creative Vocal Stroking

Other languages

If a person grew up with a different mother tongue than what you are using with them, it is harder for the newer language to penetrate back into the old memories. If you can speak in the language they heard as an infant, this is very powerful. Even if they only teach you one word or phrase to repeat, integrate this into the vocal stroking. If you happen to already know their first language, all the better.

Gibberish

Another way to work with the voice is to use gibberish, or nonsensical words. When a baby is born, they do not yet know the language, so all the words are heard as pure sound. In therapy, you can simply speak in a loving, rhythmic, caressing tone and babble in whatever way comes to you. "Sida ey nayat e conda, sayte lakuntha...." This reaches further past the conscious mind and into very primal energies and can be amazingly powerful.

Using Names, Songs, Sounds and Music

Try repeating their name in a soft voice, or singing it to them repeatedly. Use the name they had as a child.

Sound vibrations penetrate deep into all the cells, and vocal sounds have many overtones that have beneficial effects on the body and emotions. Many people sing to their children to help them sleep, and singing a lullaby or other childhood favorite might be a welcome addition to your vocal stroking. Ask your client what they prefer.

Improvising songs is also very nice, if you feel able to just make up a sleepy little tune full of sweet nothings for words, or just hum it. Another very powerful practice is toning, or humming. Since a baby only hears the sounds any way, singing and toning carries a deep vibrational healing quality.

Practice: Vocal Stroking
In pairs- take turns and practice speaking the messages to each other, modulating your voice and pacing. Read the other person's messages to them while they lie down and relax. Try singing,

humming, toning, gibberish and repeating their name, and see which one they like. Allow at least 10 minutes per person.

Freeing The Voice: Baby Power

When it is your turn to be the infant, play around with opening your voice. Our voice is our first power, and it is all we should need after birth to communicate our needs to the adults around us.

We have an incredibly flexible ability to make many different sounds. Young people begin singing and making all manner of sounds very early. A normal young person makes many sounds, frequently. They will often make the same sound over and over, exploring it deeply, learning about it.

Evidently, it is important for adults to talk baby talk back to an infant; they seem to learn how to master language better if adults echo the baby's sounds back to them.

Any painful experiences around making noise in general, being loud, breathing deeply, being heard, being free to express your true feelings and have them listened to, can end up having an inhibiting effect on your ability to sing, speak and express yourself freely. Taking the time to learn to sing can have a healing effect on whatever distress is stuck around expressing yourself.

Often we are hurt around the level of noise we make when young. Did you get told "Better to be seen and not heard"? We are told to keep our voices down, not talk back, etc. The voice is really the main tool that a baby has to control their universe and ask for what they need.   Telling someone not to use and explore this tool is essentially telling them not to be powerful, which is a central hurt in all oppression, especially young people's oppression. There are ways to allow young people to use their full voice without bothering others, such as letting them yell and play loudly in another room. There needs to be space for loudness. In counseling young children, they frequently want to make lots of noise, and enjoy it when adults are loud in playing with them (shrieking, roaring, etc.).

Practice: Exploring Sounds

Exploring the variety of sounds we can make is lots of fun. Make some sounds- how many can you make? Our voice is an incredible instrument. Try going up and down the musical scale, making random spontaneous noises, animal noises, high and low sounds, soft and loud sounds, toning, forbidden sounds. Experiment with singing, shouting, screaming, silly sounds, and weird or embarrassing sounds.

Practice: Exploring Baby Sounds

What would babies need to say? Make sounds like a very young person would: random, funny, repetitive, forceful.   Try babbling, giggling, needy crying, angry crying, fear crying, sad crying, and fussing as loud as possible.   This helps you get over the embarrassment of letting your inner child speak.

Using Sounds in Counseling Sessions

These ideas are not for Heartbeat Nurturing sessions, which do not focus so much on conversations. However they may be very useful in other kinds of sessions.

-Scan your earliest memories about singing, noise, and self expression.

-Scan what sounds upset you that young children make.

-Make loud sounds. Try to fill up the room with your sounds. Yell at someone you are mad at.

-Make silly sounds, be as ridiculous and uncontrolled as possible.

-Make the sounds you knew annoyed adults when you were young.

-Try to sing badly. Be outrageous. Ham it up. Laughing is helpful to open up your voice.

-Say whatever you feel is most forbidden. Say "Listen to me!"

Chapter 7.
Nurturing Touch for Healing

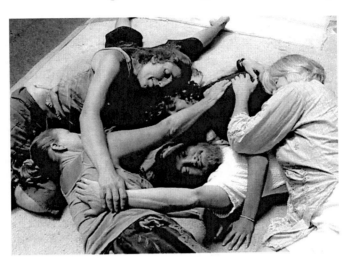

Closeness and Touching

Touch is a basic human need. People cannot normally remain emotionally healthy without close, loving physical contact with others humans regularly. This reality has been obscured in our culture. It is rare for us to get enough closeness and touching. Especially men, because boys are touched and cuddled less than girls, even from birth.

Co-counselors say everyone needs at least four hugs a day. But it needs to be quality, aware hugging. We usually have a lack of aware, non-sexual touching, especially if we don't have children or a sexual partner. Studies have shown that many older people touch pet animals far more often than other people.

Awareness means to appreciate the person you are touching fully, to be aware of how special they are as a person, and to enjoy how good it feels to touch them. Touching your client with loving awareness is a great counteraction to most people's distress.

To feel safe in receiving touch, we must know the giver is enjoying the giving. Reassure the client that you enjoy giving and being close to them. Giving is inherently enjoyable, when patterns are not blocking it. Also, it is much easier to give when the other person is really there receiving with awareness.

Practice: Your Touching Experience

Write or discuss in pairs: When and how did you get touched as a child? When and how did you touch yourself?

We accumulate blocks to touching throughout our early lives. We get painful memories from non-loving touch. What non-loving touch have you experienced? Sports? Fights? Rape or abuse, circumcision or spanking? Explore these in your sessions.

We get distress from lack of touch: How many of us were breastfed? How many feel they got adequate cuddling from parents? Were you allowed to cuddle with your friends?

These things leave distress patterns, which get in the way of fully giving and receiving touch. We may then avoid touch to avoid re-stimulating the feelings. These feelings can be expected to come up when attempting to get close to counselors or anyone. You can practice on your counselors, and let the feelings come up, and this will leave you clearer to create more warmth and closeness in your other relationships.

Also we may get the opposite pattern of craving the painful touch that we received, and seek to repeatedly act it out. We may want to be spanked or hurt by others because of the imprints of the old distress, or we may find ourselves wanting to be in the giving role. We may create relationships repeatedly where we find ourselves being abused, or we are abusing others. This is because the distress is seeking to be released and is arising to the surface to be noticed. We work on these kinds of compulsions the same way as other addictions; feel and release the feelings and do not act on them. Letting the patterns run creates more layers of hurt which must be unraveled later.

Practice: Short Session on Touch

In pairs, talk about what gets in the way of getting close to your friends for 10 minutes each. Try curling up in their lap, leaning on them, letting them put an arm around your shoulder, having them brush your hair, or laying down next to them. With a group, try a pile of people casually cuddling. What feels safe, and why?

58

Sex and Closeness

Our culture confuses sex with closeness and touching, but they are totally separate things. We can enjoy closeness with a person of any age or gender, or with animals. The great apes, our closest cousins, spend all day grooming each other. The need for closeness is a very large, daily need.

Western society places a very strong emphasis on sex. It has become something both very forbidden and yet very desirable. This love-hate attitude about sex means that there is a huge amount of attention put on it, either trying to get it or trying to avoid it. Advertising media rely heavily on sexual messages. It is separated from daily life, made mysterious and mythologized.

Deep distress about sex and closeness is widespread, and centuries old. We inherited many instincts from times before our rational mind was fully developed, such as the fight or flight reaction, and sexual impulses. There were complex systems of triggers, such as visual cues, smells, etc that would set off the rigid behavior patterns in pre-humans to insure that reproduction of the species happened.

In general, now these instinctual responses can be subordinated to the thinking mind. Rather than just act blindly on a feeling or instinct, we want to be able to think flexibly and make appropriate choices in each situation. Our reality is too complex to follow reptilian brain urges to fight or have sex.

However, often sex is the only accessible place for people to get any small bit of their huge daily, rational needs met for closeness, touching, love and for discharge also. We may think we want sex when we actually want some of these other needs filled.

Practice: Aware Cuddling

When you make love, what is it that you hope to feel, that makes sex really special and good? Do you get enough of it? With your lover, try cuddling and giving each other attention and aware touch for 15 to 30 minutes minimum. Enjoy sexuality later, and feel the difference.

In people who have worked extensively on their sexuality, or grown up in relatively distress-free situations, sex becomes something much less important when all the other needs for closeness, love, etc are really fulfilled. It is still a very beautiful and wonderful thing to share, and the desperation and need often felt around it are greatly reduced.

In Heartbeat Nurturing, we are working directly with physical closeness near the heart and breasts. In the advanced practice, we are actually suckling. So we are likely to bring forward sexual feelings and longings, in either the giver or the receiver. This will not be an issue for lovers doing an exchange, but may need some careful discernment between others. In general, our intention is to exchange nurturing and closeness, so if sexual feelings arise, it is recommended to finish the therapy session, wait a while, and to have a sexual encounter later if you so choose. We will discuss that more in Chapter 11.

Types and Effects of Touch

The intention behind the touching has a huge effect on the feeling of the person receiving, and also the amount of actual attention that is focused by the giver during the touching. So we want to play with two aspects of touch: the actual quality of the physical touch, and the mental intention and attention that is happening.

The different kinds of physical touch create very different responses. In general, we want to touch each other in these sessions as a loving parent handling a delicate infant. So our touches will usually be light and slow stroking, and firm comforting holding.

Practice: Physical Touching Styles
Experiment with different qualities of physical touching: fast. slow, deep, light, soft fingertips only, deep pressure on one point, squeezing, kneading, tapping, shaking, slapping, stroking. Try them on yourself and notice what you prefer. Try them with a partner and ask them frequently for feedback.

Practice: Attitudes While Touching
Touch your own feet or a friend's in different ways: in a businesslike way, in a distracted way, in a nurturing way, in a sensual way. Notice the differences.

As much as possible, our attitude will stay focused on enjoyment and admiration of the one we are holding. We will be focusing on giving them our full attention, and keeping other thoughts about the future and past out of our minds. If you find your mind wandering as a therapist, it is likely that you are triggered, so just notice that and do your best to pull yourself back to the present moment. Being present for another is definitely ad skill that can be practiced and learned.

Practice: Nurturing Touch
What touch makes you feel most nurtured? Ask for it specifically and receive it from a friend or counselor.

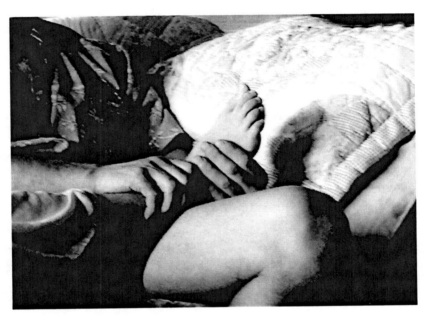

Getting Comfortable Cradling an Adult

Cradling is when we are holding someone in our arms, in a way that helps them feel wrapped in love, nurtured and safe.

In most therapeutic situations, cradling is not an option because of legalities and professional boundaries. Certainly suckling is not usually in the realm of what is acceptable for professional therapy, except perhaps for sex therapists or surrogates. So the experience of being closely cradled generally needs to be given in peer counseling situations where no money is exchanged.

There are a few tricky things about cradling an adult, because they are big! It is relatively easy to hold a small infant, but how to we create a similar feeling while holding someone who may be larger that we are? There are a few challenges emotionally as well, and those are explored in Chapter 11.

Different positions work better for some people than others. The best thing to do is experiment for a few minutes before you start the relaxation and induction.

Things to keep in mind are that you want to be able to hold them for a while, so get comfortable with pillows and arm supports. In all cases, you want enough softness and padding. Decide if you want to be on a bed, a couch or a large chair, or a pad on the floor.

Since the session involves some time where they are relaxed after you finish with the closeness, it is best to have a way to lay them down away from your body if possible. This gives them a time of coming back inside themselves and into their own center, so they do not have an abrupt disconnection.

We want them to be able to hear the heartbeat, so that usually means them leaning across your body, with their body on your right, leaning across to hear your heart on your left shoulder.

You can decide whether the giver wants to sit or lay down, and whether the receiver will be between their legs or to one side.

Energy Wrapping

Another visualization to use during cradling is imagining that you are wrapping the client in a warm blanket of energy, extending from your heart and through your arms. Enfold them with a golden sweet feeling of loving kindness. If you do not know the person well, think of how you feel about someone you care about, and expand that feeling in your heart.

Synchronized Breathing

Breathing with the client is a wonderful way to attune to their energy and bring yourself into harmonic resonance with them. Track their breathing and breathe in and out at the same time, during the time you are not talking or singing.

Heartbeat Listening

Hearing the heartbeat is a very powerful relaxation method, and has been studied extensively. As an adult, we rarely have a chance to relax and hear someone's heartbeat, partly because we usually relax alone, or sleep at the same time. Having your head on someone's chest is not such a comfortable sleeping position. Even when we are being sexual and close, our ear is usually not in the correct position very long to hear the heartbeat. So it is a real treat to be able to relax and hear the heart for a longer time period.

Practice: Cradling a Partner

Invite a partner to put their head on your heart. Find the most comfortable position so the heartbeat can be heard. Softly stroke the face and shoulders, while in silence, for at least 5 minutes. Imagine wrapping them with your loving energy, and synchronize breathing. Keep your attention focused on loving them. Then trade.

Chapter 8.
Getting Your Energy Clear- Preparations for the Therapist

If you take a few minutes before giving a session to clear and ground yourself, you will greatly improve the experience for you and your client. They will help keep your mind clear and focused in present time, and your heart open. After the session, you may want and need to clear yourself again, so that you can continue on with your life without a lot of concern or attachment to the client's experience.

These meditation practices are also useful to do with the client after a session, to help integrate and clear their energies. A lot of this information came from my training at the Berkeley Psychic Institute, during the early 1980's. I have been finding it useful ever since then.

Matter and Energy

All matter is energy, but there are different levels of vibration, in a spectrum; some finer and faster, some dense and slow. We have many different levels of being- the dense physical form, the less dense (but still weighty) emotions, the finer level of thoughts, and still finer essence of our souls or spirits; our pure consciousness.

We have many "bodies", one for each level, which can be seen psychically as overlapping layers of an energy field or aura. They get lighter and lighter as you move out farther from the physical body.

The physical is the most solid. But even matter, on the atomic level, has more space in it than substance. The fast movement of the atoms gives the illusion of solidity, like the turning blades of an electric fan seem to become a solid wheel. Science is not even really sure if there is such a thing as a particle, since atomic bodies act just as much like waves of energy as anything else.

Our attention or consciousness is not limited to our physical bodies. We often leave our bodies, as in sleeping. Wherever your attention is, that is where you are as a being. Your spiritual essence as a being is a pure point of awareness. When you are paying attention to what you will do next week, or what you did in the past, part of your energy or being goes there.

If your energy is always centered on the mental levels of planning for the future, you are not present in the physical present time reality. It draws you out of what is happening here and now, which, after all, is really where the action is. When we experience hurtful events that are then unhealed and unresolved, part of our psychic energy gets "stuck" there in the past, until healing occurs.

Most people are "out" of their physical body a lot; thinking of faraway places, being centered in their head only (thinking), spiritually asleep, or feeling the body is ugly or bad, or avoiding physical pain or boredom. A lot of people eat without really being present, so they tend to overeat, because they are not really tasting it or noticing they are full.

Make the Body Safe and Loved

The physical body has it's own consciousness. In fact, every cell of the body has its own kind of awareness. A physical body is like a huge city, with millions of little beings, (cells, bacteria, etc.), making it work, doing their different jobs. It is an expression of, and a reflection of, your state of consciousness and your spiritual being. A body is very wise- it knows exactly what it needs for healing at all times. It will keep working- breathing, heart pumping, etc. even when the being is not paying much attention to it. But if the connection gets too remote, illness and death result.

But when you are not in your body much, the body doesn't feel very safe, kind of like an abandoned child. The energy field around it becomes weak and flat. It needs love and attention from your spirit, because the spirit is the source of life energy for the body. The connection or bridge between the spirit and the body is the breath. Life energy is brought to the body mainly via the breath. The body can only live a few minutes without breath. Learning to breathe properly can change your entire mental and emotional state.

When doing meditation and healing, if the body isn't safe, It won't allow you to be aware of subtle energies. The emotions or physical pains will clamor too loudly and drown out the quieter voices. This is why it is hard to know what your guidance is, or what is the right thing to do, when you are upset.

In our culture, we are taught to identify with our body as being the most real part of ourselves. This belief leads to our fear of death, because we identify as being only the body. At the same time, our culture discounts the physical body as being bad, gross, something with passions that need to be controlled. We hide it with clothes, and hide it's natural functions as shameful.

What effects does this have? Although being out of our body reduces pain and bring detachment, it makes us feel unstable, with our energy diffused. We feel vulnerable to attack, awkward, off-balance, unaware, ineffective.

We need to reclaim our love for our bodies, learn what is needed to be healthy, and care for them as a best friend or a child. One thing our bodies need is to be grounded, and feel connected to the earth. Anytime you feel scared, you are probably not well grounded.

We want to learn to bring the vibrations of loving consciousness into the body, and to re-tune the body's energy systems to be accustomed to finer energies. Our bodies are very flexible, and able to adapt to a wide range of vibration. In doing meditation, we are actually raising our vibrational level. If you get the vibration fast enough, disease organisms can't live. The slower vibrations of microbes can't exist in a strong, higher field.

People who have a lot of life force running through their bodies are more resistant to disease. Other things that raise the vibration are exercise, oxygen, occasional fasting, avoiding animal and low quality foods, laughing, singing, sexual energy, and healing old emotional blocks.

69

When we bring our consciousness into the body, we are able to focus our energies to move the world around us, and create our own lives. This body, here and now, is the point in the universe that you have to work with, that is all your own. The more you are in your body, the more you have real power in this world available to you. You can also separate your own energy and problems from other people, since you are better aware of your own physical boundaries.

Grounding

What does grounding mean? Making the body feel more real, putting your attention on the physical body, and strengthening the energy connection between your body and the earth.

Psychic energy follows the same laws of physical energy- energy flows long the path of least resistance. In electricity, outlets are grounded with a wire to allow any surges of power to bleed off harmlessly.

We experience surges of psychic energy also; as in shocks, someone getting upset with us or attacking, or loud noises that set off our "fight or flight" adrenal responses. When energy gets stuck in us, it hurts. If it has somewhere to flow out to, a large surge is not uncomfortable.

Grounding Visualization

Close your eyes, take a deep breath. Your brain needs oxygen for energy. It takes no effort to visualize; thoughts are so light, just relax.

Imagine a cylindrical tube attached to your pelvis, going down into the ground. It can be a pipeline, a hose, a tube, a root or a tree trunk. On an exhale, imagine it sinking, falling easily, getting longer and longer, falling though all the layers of the earth, rocks, water, lava, all the way down to the very center of the earth. Imagine it is very solid. It winds around the center of the earth, getting firmly attached. You can imagine a heavy ball or rock dropping down, and that may make it easier.

Where is there tension or pain in your body? Relax and drain out that excess energy. Breathing at the same time will help a lot. Gather the energy into a ball or blob on the inhale, then let it drop on the exhale.

Breathe, stretch, drop over so your arms dangle to the floor, let your head be loose, and let any energy that may have been stuck in your head drain out the top. The body accumulates excess energy during the day unless it is grounded. Try taking a grounding break a few times a day when you are tired. A good time is when sitting on a toilet for a few minutes or while driving.

It is important to get your body used to this new feeling, so practice grounding. Especially, ground before a hard demanding task, or stressful situation.

Practice: Grounding

Practice for five minutes, sitting. Then bend over and drain out. How do you feel?

Try grounding your car, your house, your bedroom. Just imagine a grounding cord as wide as the object you are grounding. There are no limits in the thought realm.

Stand up, and practice grounding. Walk around. Keep your attention on your grounding cord. How does it feel different than usual?

Centering and Filling Visualization

Ground again. Breathe. Touch the sides of your head, and allow yourself to be right in the center of your head, as though you are looking out of your eyes like they were windows. This is a place of power, known as the third eye. From here, you can be very aware, and powerful in creating your life the way you want it.

If ever you are spaced out and you want to come back to the present, touch your head, breathe, ground, and pull yourself in to the center of your head.

You can also center by focusing on one of the other chakras, such as the heart center or the belly, or the feet, or the entire spine. Each one has its own benefits. The heart center is a good place to be during a Heartbeat session, as it encourages feelings of love and connection. The lower belly is used extensively in the martial arts, as it provides a strong sense of physical stability.

Call all your scattered energy back from all the places you have left it. Places like other people's problems you have been trying to solve, your own problems, your work, places you have been, your creative projects, or the fantasy worlds of books and movies. Pull it in like a magnet, focusing on the inhale. As it comes back, it becomes neutral, clear, and bright. Let it be cleaned of all qualities or impressions.

Then, as you inhale, let it wash through your body, shining down and all through you, washing away whatever you don't need now. Really absorb as much of it as you can. It is a gift to yourself. Refill yourself. It is good to always refill whenever you drain energy out. Nature abhors a vacuum, even on an energy level. Fill the emptiness with what you want, with light, love and vibrant life

We usually leave a bit our energy everywhere we put our attention. The more attention you pay to something, the more of your energy is there. We can get "strung out" or "spread too thin" when we have a lot going on. Leaving a bit of your attention on something is like leaving open a communication line, like a phone off the hook. If you get too many of these, it's overwhelming.

We have an infinite amount of energy as a being, but often we forget to recharge ourselves by drawing in more.

Practice: Centering Walks
As you walk, inside or out, place your attention on different areas and breathe into them. Try the third eye area between the forehead. Then the heart. Then just your feet. Then the lower belly, known as the Hara center. Then your entire spine. What do you feel?

72

Clearing and Purification

Clearing yourself is easier when you relax. Just put your attention on yourself, and give to yourself, filling up with your own highest energy. Other energies will be naturally pushed out.

If you have trouble clearing out a person or some energy, look to see how you are attached to it, or holding it to you somehow. Are you curious or interested in them? Are you holding a grudge or trying to control somehow? Trying to avoid looking at something by pushing it away? Feeling responsible? All these things will make it hard to be detached and clear. Notice that you can pick up all your concerns and attachments again later, if you want them. Just for now, let them go. Again, notice the sense of lightness, expansion and quiet emptiness.

Clearing can be done using physical means, also. Water is especially effective at clearing away old energy. Taking a shower also cleans the aura. Washing your hands after healing work, with cold water, is a good idea.

You can use your hands to pull energy out of the aura, or simply to massage it out of muscles. Crying and other emotional release clears the aura. Shaking, stretching, and dancing all clear energy out.

Cleansing with fire: Native people use smudging with sage smoke, imagining the negative energies being carried away in the smoke. A sweat lodge is a powerful purification ritual, and fasting.

Using earth: Lying on the ground, or in a mud bath. Being in nature will purify our thoughts and bodies. Walking barefoot.

Cleansing with air: Deep breaths! Standing in the wind.

Think of the ways that you use now to clear yourself.

Practice: Clearing

Ground yourself, and center. On an exhale, imagine that everything you don't need right now, all thoughts, energies or pain that is not in harmony with your own highest good, is loosening up and draining down your grounding cord. You could try imagining unplugging tendrils of cords from your energy body that represent attachments or old patterns.

Say to yourself: "I now release anyone else's energy that I may be holding on to. It is free to go back to the people it belongs to." Other affirmations may help, such as "I now let go and trust that all is taken care of." "I turn it over to God."

On the exhale, imagine lumps of colored energy around you loosening and falling into the ground, or drifting off into space and dispersing. Feel yourself becoming more and more empty and clear. Breathe in to the open, clear space around you.

Aura Sweeping

Auras are simply the electro-magnetic and spiritual energy field that you radiate. Whatever you are feeling and thinking is reflected in your aura. It can appear to have separate layers, or be blotchy and chaotic. It is always changing rapidly, as the person's mood changes. It gets more and more light and refined the farther out from your body it goes. We have very subtle layers of the aura that go out for miles. You might feel them in a large city, the dense, crowded feeling of all those auras, and other electromagnetic fields.

In pairs, have one person sit in a straight-backed chair, feet flat on floor, hands on thighs, palms up. This allows energy to flow freely, open and receptive. They can just relax, do not have to meditate or run energy, although grounding is always a good idea.

Practice: Aura Sweeps

Open your hand chakras by imagining a bright little sun in your palms, getting larger, or a door opening wider. Start out above the head, and about 6 inches away from another person's body with your fingers extended. Comb down through the aura from top to bottom, smoothing out the edges. It may feel like heat, coolness, pressure or magnetism. This is the edge of a layer of their aura. Does it change as you go up or down the body? Is it stronger some places then others? Use neutral, cosmic energy, pulled in from the universal

74

pool of energy, clean and clear. Shake your fingers out, and drain the cleared energy out.

The Torus Healing Meditation

The toroid shape or "torus" (a form like the outside of a donut) has many special properties. It allows energy to spiral inwards and outwards on the same surface, creating a connected, holographic form. It is the template for the physical universe, and the natural form of the flow of electromagnetic energy. The electromagnetic fields of the earth and of the human body move in this shape. The human brain has neurosynaptic connections in the form of a torus, as are blood cells and atoms, cyclones, hurricanes and many forms of plant life.

This shape can be used to generate higher electromagnetic current in your body, creating better health. All cells have a small magnetic field and all nerves work through electrical impulses. The technique of using a weak magnetic current for healing illness and killing viruses and parasites is being widely used with great beneficial effects.

Working with the torus shape in meditation can have quick and powerful effects on the mind and body.

Get into any position, lying or standing or sitting, where the feet and hands are not touching each other but are resting separately.

Leaving the hands and feet open creates a stronger energy exchange with the natural forces of life in the sky and earth. It can be done sitting cross-legged with hands on knees, but this will lessen the grounding effect of the flow through the legs. A more open pose of sitting on a chair with feet flat on the ground might be preferable.

On an in-breath, imagine lines of energy beginning to flow up from your feet (if you are standing or lying) or below your pelvis (if sitting cross-legged), up through your central core. As you exhale they flow up and out through the top of your head to a couple of feet above your head, and down around your body on all sides.

These lines are small but potent streams of energy and magnetic force, which can be visualized as iridescent filaments, the way a human hair looks when it turns to rainbows in the sun. There are many of these tiny strands – at least one every one half inch all around the body, at a distance of 1 meter or 3 feet. It is about the distance of your fingertips when you extend your arms out to the sides and above your head.

As you breathe in from a few feet around you, you are activating the flow of vibration on the outer edge of your individual aura. This is the magnetic field that sustains your body, emotions and mind. There are more subtle layers of your aura, which are further from your body, but they do not relate so much to you as an individual soul. This meditation is about who you are, in your individual personality and body.

The iridescent filaments converge in your center and continue out the top of your head and fountain out like a spray of water in all directions, to travel back down on all sides as you exhale. They form a continuous loop that forms a torus, or the shape of the outline of a doughnut. Add to the energy flow by squeezing your perineum muscles while inhaling.

Every time the energy rises up, it rotates just slightly in a clockwise direction. So if there was a little ball riding on the flow, it would move slightly to your right every time it traveled up and down with the breath while it was in front of you, and left when it got around to the back. It would actually be moving in a very tightly bound spiral, which is what all the energy is doing.

Pains and illness exist where energy is blocked or tangled, and has lost its rhythmic pattern. Imagine these healing lines of force like tiny beams, which penetrate the tissues that are out of alignment. As they penetrate the painful areas, they create a magnetic pull, like a small trickle of water through the mud. With every breath the blocked area becomes more porous and loose, as the energy streams wear away at blocks and realign the flows. Relax as deeply as possible, letting the body open and wash away the toxins and illness.

Separating Your Energy From Others

Why would you want to separate from others? Aren't we already so isolated?

On this personality level, of being individual people, we are not set up to totally blend into each other. You can't have two bodies in one space at the same time, and each body is completely unique in the universe. On the level we work with in daily life, it is good to know your boundaries, so that you know what is your own, totally unique energy. No one else is exactly you. No one else can know how best to live your life. You are the most important person in your own universe.

Sometimes we want to be able to pull back into ourselves and just be in our own energy. This is especially important if you have just been doing healing work with someone, and you have been in deep rapport. It is helpful to pull back and remember that you are a different person, so that you don't walk away trying to solve all their problems, or with the symptoms of their physical pain.

Visualization: Owning Your Body and Personal Space

Ground and center. Get a sense of the space your body is taking up. Remember you have a right to be here, taking up space on the earth plane. Feel the space about two feet all around you, above and under.

Ground your entire space, making your grounding cord as large as your aura, all around your body.

Own your body, and your space. Claim it; this is mine! It is really the only part of the universe that is totally, 100% yours. Settle down into it, like sitting into a chair. Be in your toes. How are they feeling? Fill them up with your being, say hello to them. Be in your feet, how are they feeling? Now your lower legs. Relax each part as you go.

Fill them up with your conscious attention. Attention/consciousness is power, is love, is healing. Just paying attention to something often heals it. Let every part of your body be filled with your being/attention. Think: this is my body, my best friend. Mine alone.

Be aware of any part that is uncomfortable, or weak, and say Hello, what are you trying to tell me? Listen receptively. You may get an image, a sentence, a color. Have a conversation with the body part. How do you feel about it? Writing this down may be helpful.

Just for contrast, try being somewhere else. Imagine a beautiful place you have been before, and see it on your mind's screen. Feel the air on your skin, smell the smells of that place, hear the sounds. Now come back here, but imagine you are floating in one of the corners of the room, looking down on everyone. You can see your body sitting there, and everyone else's. What does it look like from up there?

Now come back to being right in your center. How is it different? Breathe, bend over, clear out.

If you find you are having any of the following symptoms following a session (or anytime really) it can mean that you need more separation of energies: confusion, or unusual/unfamiliar body aches and pains, obsession with the other person and her/his problems. It can be helpful to consciously focus on pulling your own energy back into your body, and separating from the other person.

We have the most fun in relationships if both of us have a strong, positive sense of self, and then we can dance and play side by

78

side. It is easy to see why you wouldn't want some one's negative energy. How do you feel after someone has thrown you a bunch of angry energy?

Even positive energy from other people, when you hold onto it, clutters up your space, like knick-knacks or keepsakes. It is hard to create, to be free, if you have lots of other people's concepts of who you are (expectations, concerns, needs, etc.) in your space. It can work better to let their loving energy go through you, enjoy it and let it heal you and then flow on.

Practice: Separating Your Energy

Own your body, and your space. Claim it; this is mine! It is really the only part of the universe that is totally, 100% yours. Imagine that you are pulling back all your scattered energy. Tuck yourself back into your body the way you would settle into a chair. From this position, let go of any energy that you may be holding of others, and let it return to them. Notice five ways that you are different from the other person. Remind yourself that their problems are not yours to solve. You can still love and appreciate them, from a neutral place. Breathe, bend over, clear out.

If it still seems hard to let go of them, imagine them standing in front of you. Say "Hello" and ask them to leave your space. Imagine the image of them getting smaller and smaller until it is gone in the distance.

If you are having difficulty separating from another person, you may still be attached to them in some way. Perhaps you are curious about them; trying to learn something from them; or they remind you of parts of your own life. Take the time to examine these possibilities, then, let go of them and try the separation techniques again.

Whenever you are confused, you probably have other energies in your space. Other voices are drowning out the quiet inner voice of your guidance. When you are grounded and centered, you always know what is the right thing to do, and what is your own truth.

Notice when you are in your space, and when you are out, and when other people are in or out of their bodies. Notice where you are when you are working, when eating, or when driving. If you aren't in your own space, here & now, where are you?

79

Handling Negative Energy

What about when someone is sending you negative energy, or attacking you? This is a sign that they are hurting and need help and love. They may have feedback for you that is valuable, but that can be given in a loving way. If they are sending you hateful energy, they are showing you their wounds. If you can manage to stay in neutral, and return loving energy to them, it will often completely change your relationship.

In this case, doing a love healing meditation can be very effective. When meditating, imagine an image of the person you are having difficulty with. Surround the image with love and light. Imagine seeing them as their soul is, beyond all the patterns of ego and negativity. Communicate directly with who they really are; an infinite being of light and peace. Making this connection inside yourself will help you both to have a clear and loving connection externally.

Practice: Staying Neutral

Visualize your body, well grounded, becoming completely transparent. Like glass, or air. All energies thrown at you will go right through, or around you, with nothing to latch on to.

Imagine a scene when someone throws some energy at you, which is called a whack. It can be anger, sexual energy, fear, need, whatever. It could be any strong feeling or expectation. Watch the energy go right through you, or around you.

What are some charged sentences that always bug you? Imagine people saying them, and let them go through.

Imagine different emotions coming to the surface (happiness, anger, sadness, fear, distain) Stay in neutral, grounded, with a body of air. Observe the emotion, and drain it out your grounding cord.

Opening to Channel Healing

No one can heal anyone else, unless they allow it. Really, the other person is using the healer as a way to draw their own healing energy to them. Thus it is important to remain detached from the results of any healing attempt. Sometimes the person receiving will be ready to change, and sometimes they won't. Sometimes they may feel temporarily worse, as old pain gets stirred up and transformed. Stay detached and loving, and have faith that your good intentions to be helpful will help create whatever the person needs right then.

Never take credit for healing someone. Think of yourself as only a channel for the energy to be drawn through. The more you can get your adult self out of the way, the more your channels will be open

Staying in a neutral inner space while doing any kind of healing work is important. Sometimes people will project onto you all the bad feelings that may be getting stirred up during the healing, and even accuse you of hurting them. Do not become defensive in this case, but simply restate your desire to be helpful and loving, and apologize for anything you may have done that was not helpful.

We have important energy centers, called chakras, in our hands, which relate to our ability to do things, manipulate our world. We use these a lot in healing work. We will practice opening and cleaning them

Another way to open them is to rub them together quickly, increasing the heat and circulation and therefore the sensitivity. Some people will be more able to feel these energies than others, so keep trying if you do not feel much on the first try.

Practice: *Opening The Hand Chakras*

To open the hands, sit up straight with eyes closed, ground and run your energy. After a moment, begin to pay attention to your hands, to the palms. Imagine little swirling currents of light begin to get stronger. Or imagine a lens opening, letting a bright ball of energy grow bigger. On an exhale, breathe a flow of energy into your hands. It takes no effort. Opening them consists of relaxing, not tensing up.

Practice: *Energy Balls*

When they feel fairly open, bring your palms facing each other but not touching. Maybe about 6 inches apart. Begin to breath into the space between them, imagining a ball of bright light there. With every breath it gets brighter. Make a small patting motion with your hands to feel the magnetic feeling better. When you sense the ball strongly, try stretching it. How far can you move your hands apart and still feel it? What happens when you bring them back together?

Opening the Heart Channel

Once you feel your hands warm and open, you can connect them with the energy center in your heart. The heart creates the strongest magnetic field in the body. You can learn to choose when you want to open your heart and generate loving feelings, just like learning to tune a

81

dial on the radio. Once the heart energy is open, we will breathe it through the breasts and arms to the client.

Energy Wrapping

An important visualization to use during cradling, as we said earlier, is imagining that you are wrapping the client in a warm blanket of energy, extending from your heart and through your arms. Enfold them with a golden blanket of energy. If you are working with someone in a workshop you don't know well, and have trouble feeling love for someone on demand, think of how you feel about someone you care about, or a pet, or a beautiful place, and expand that feeling in your heart.

More power can be generated for the wrapping if you use the energy in the root center, by squeezing the perineal muscles around the genitals, and breathing upward into the heart and out the arms.

Practice: Opening the Heart Channel

Imagine an image of the person you love, and remember what you love and appreciate about them. Stay focused on the positive, even if negative thoughts arise about them. Increase the intensity of the love feelings, and as you exhale, breathe out a stream of warmth energy to them. Imagine it strengthening and helping them.

Channeling the Divine- Getting out of the Way

The task of the therapist and Priest/ess is to step from the adult ego and conscious personality, into the Deeper/Divine self, at will. It is letting go of who you think you are and melting into something bigger. And before we can do that effectively, we need to know our ego selves well.

Everyone has their own energy vibration, which is unique and distinctive and is constantly changing and fluctuating. The changes correspond to our emotions, physical health and thoughts.

Getting to know and recognize your own vibration is very important. Many of us automatically take on the vibration of whomever we are with, unconsciously. This is a way of matching energy.

The positive effect of matching energy is to give us a feeling of closeness, sameness, and harmony, of rapport. It can be a way of learning, a way of trying out new levels of being. This can be used as a spiritual practice, which Sufis call *Fana*, or effacement, in which you seek to totally absorb yourself in a certain vibration, thus losing the awareness of yourself as a separate ego entity.

The negative effects of unconsciously matching energy can include giving up your own space and power, getting confused, and being unable to tell what is you and what is the other person. Or being pulled down to a less healthy vibration than you were on before. It can be a problem for healers, who sometimes end up taking on the symptoms of their patients. If you are experiencing any of these things, pull your energy back to your center, ground, and own your space.

Examine why you might be pulled to match people unconsciously. Some of us learned to do it as a survival skill around unsafe people, or to try to rescue others, or as a way to feel close.

For healing work, it is best to be on a faster, and yet harmonic vibrational level. It is easier to see another person clearly when you are not exactly on their same level. The person who wants healing is helped by being around your energy, and by absorbing it or matching it. This is how a lot of spiritual teaching happens; the students absorb a certain vibration from the teacher.

A distressed client is not helped if you let yourself get pulled into their less healthy energy. Remember that jumping in with a drowning person and endangering yourself will not help them. To be a healer you must be able to maintain your own high energy level while surrounded by denser energies. That is why it is important not to try to heal while you are ill or weak.

Visualization: Matching and Un-matching Energy

First, be in your own energy right now. Ground, center, own your space, clear. Notice another person, and try to feel what their vibration is. What color, texture, sound is it? How do you feel looking at them from your own level?

Now try to match their energy. Get on the same level as they are. Follow them as they walk, and try to walk in exactly the same way. How do you feel now, emotionally and physically? How do you feel toward them? Just notice how it feels.

Now change your energy level to a healing level. Open yourself to let the healing energy of life run through you. Perhaps you want to imagine running gold or white energy through you. Or some other color that feels harmonious with their energy, but more refined. Or you might imagine a healing sound in you. How does it feel to perceive them now?

Practice: Tuning Your Energy

Try running different types of energy through you. Try different colors, tones or textures. How do you feel with each color? Chant Om or Ah on different notes, and feel the differences.

Imagine matching energy with high beings like angels, Christ, or specific Gods or Goddesses (Mary, Kuan yin, Venus, Pan, Buddha, Abraham). Each of them has a special vibration which can be tuned in to at will. Imagine letting them come through you. This is what people do when they channel. This practice will help refine your energies, and can be healing physically as well.

Chapter 9.
Invoking the Divine

Tuning to the Divine Creator/Parent

The specific energy that we wish to invoke in these sessions is that of the Divine Parent, either in male of female form, or a more androgynous form. The word that was used by Jesus in his native tongue of Aramaic was *Abwoon,* which means simply the nurturing Parent, and has no gender identity. Each person has both male and female qualities, in different amounts. We usually experience parents with strong gender identity and sex role patterning, so it is useful to think about the energies of mothering and fathering, and what they mean to you.

Practice: Discussion of Parents
What is mothering energy? What is fathering? What is the difference? Which one do you crave the most? Why?

Opening to the Mother

What is your concept of the Divine Feminine? How do perceive it in this world, and how to do you feel about Her? Often in our culture we are not brought up thinking about the Divine as feminine, but rather as a fathering energy. Yet in early history, the foundations of spiritual expression invariably involved a Goddess. LIke the younger inner self, our feminine self is often oppressed and discounted as having little worth. We have to reclaim and heal that part of ourselves. Finding your own inner Goddess is a magical, transformative path.

Practice: Mothering History
Mini session listening trade for 10-15 minutes each: How were you mothered? How open are you to being mothered now? Is it easy to mother someone else?

Aspects of the Goddess

The feminine energy manifests as many different forms, the most classic being Maiden, Mother, Queen, Crone and Protectress. Ancient religions had many Goddesses who personified these energies. They are deep archetypes in our psyche and can be powerful to work with. The Maiden is the energy of the young woman, the virgin, the playful innocent girl. The Mother is the round fullness of a pregnant mother, like the full moon. The Queen expresses the time when a woman has really come into her own power, freedom and creativity. The Crone is the wise old woman, the grandmother. The Protectress or Huntress is the warrior Goddess, who defends the weak and stands up for what is right.

Practice: Goddess Walk
Walk around the room as though you are each of those aspects: Maiden, Mother, Queen, Crone, Protectress. Move your body with each energy. How does it feel? Which one feels more easy and familiar? Which is harder?

After you have done a relaxation and regression in a session, you may want to bring this next meditation in as well. Some people are less inclined to the spiritual aspect, so just decide what is right for you. You can also practice this alone, or with a recording.

Meditation- Meeting the Mother Goddess

As you lay there in your infant body, feel a huge warmth surround you, and feel as though very large warm arms are enfolding you. You are held close next to soft and full breasts, and you hear a heart beating. You know that you are cherished as a most precious child, a jewel, a treasure.

The mother Goddess wants all good things for you, wants you to have every desire fulfilled, every comfort, always surrounded by love and abundance. Breathe deeply and allow this generous loving energy to come into you. More than you ever have before. Let her nurture you. You deserve it. You are her child, her own creation.

She offers you her huge warm breast, and you open your mouth and feel the sweetest energy in the world coming in to you, filling your heart and belly. It is pure and clean, and totally satisfying, like nectar. She has more than enough, and she wants to give you as much as you want. Let yourself take everything you want, as much as you want.

She has more than you could possibly every need, to take all that you need. It is your right to be filled, to be whole, to be loved.

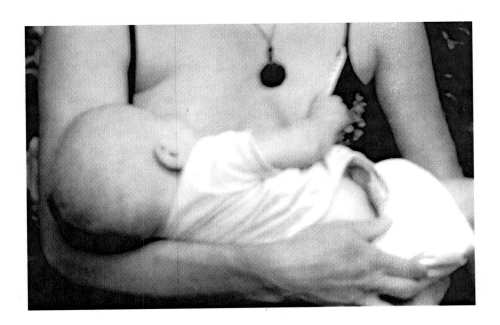

Opening to The Father

In this age of absentee fathers, many of us find ourselves feeling bereft and confused about father energy. What is it to be a good father? How many of us have role models of devoted, caring fathers?

Our culture has lost the customs and traditions that helped young men transition into their manhood, leaving an emptiness. Male bonding is difficult to find in many families, because of the way that boys are hurt and conditioned. Men are encouraged to shut down and not feel their feelings at an early age; to be tough, competitive and independent. Boy babies are not touched as much as girls, so they often grow up feelings a deep longing for closeness.

They are never supposed to show weakness or need. Men are in the role of oppressors in our society, and often feel guilt about that role they have been trained to do.

Practice: Fathering History
Mini session listening trade for 10-15 minutes each: How were you fathered? How open are you to being fathered now? Is it easy to father someone else?

Finding our inner loving male energy, and specifically our fathering energy, is important and healing. It often involves letting go of our training about what men are and should be. It can involve giving up performing and pretending to be perfect. It might look like reaching out and connecting and being real. For men, letting go of the adult self can be particularly hard. Letting yourself feel and act like an infant can be terrifying, or almost like dying of embarrassment.

Men often have resistance to letting another man father them in Heartbeat Therapy, because of homophobic issues. It is rare in our culture that men touch at all, much less embrace for an extended time. However if they can allow it to happen, it can be deeply moving and profoundly healing. It is extra important to do the relaxation and regression in this case, to help the men let go and forget that they are grown up men.

88

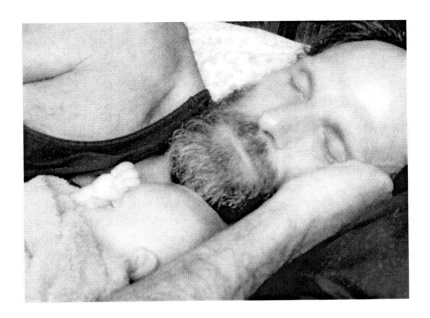

It is very important for the man giving the fathering to be present and confident, and loving. Imagine your self as an aspect of the Divine Masculine helps to bring you more inner power, so you have more to give. The father shows up in different forms, and the archetypes are often: Protector, Nurturer, Teacher, King, Servant.

Practice: Walking the Father

Take on the energy of the Father in different forms: Protector, Nurturer, Teacher, King, Servant. Walk and move with them. Which one feels more easy and familiar? Which is harder?

Meditation- Meeting the Inner Divine Father

As you lay there in your infant body, feel a huge warmth surround you, and feel as though very large warm arms are enfolding you. You are held close next to a strong muscular chest, and you hear a heart beating. You might feel the hairs on his chest and arms. You know you are completely safe. You know that you are cherished as a most precious child, a jewel, a treasure. The father wants all good things for you, and wants to be close to you. He wants for you to be protected, and always surrounded by love and abundance. Breathe deeply and allow this generous loving energy to come into you. More than you ever have before. Let him nurture you. You deserve it. You are his child, his own creation, and he is proud of you. You can completely relax and let go, and he will take care of you.

Elements of Ritual

Creating a Sacred Context

A sacred space is a time outside of normal daily life, when our usual personality is set aside and we relax and let go of control. Change happens best in altered states of consciousness, and there are many ways to create those states. Basically we want to make it clear to ourselves that the session is a time where we can let go of being our normal selves, and set into something different where magic can happen.

Doing ritual actions and ceremonies helps to create this feeling of safety and special focus. We will do many things comfortably in a ritual context that we would not do ordinarily. For example, many people go to church, and kneel to pray. They might feel very strange kneeling in a humble manner outside the church service.

The process can be done without the spiritual context, but we have found that it adds greatly to the effectiveness of the sessions, and helps reduce transference problems.

There a few elements that are found in most ceremonies and rituals, in one form or another. Even business meetings may go through some of these steps. The steps are: purification & blessing, setting intent, grounding, making the container, invoking larger energies, doing the main work, closing the ritual, clearing the space and yourself.

Blessings

Blessings help us remember our sacredness, and are a statement of our intention to be clear and open to love and healing. You might use smudging or incense, anointing with an essential oil, water blessing, or holding or using crystals. You can also do blessings by bowing to each other and appreciating each other's presence.

Grounding

Sitting together in meditation, connecting to the earth energy, deep slow breathing, and eye contact are all good ways to ground. This step also helps to match energy and attune to each other.

Making the Container

Visualize a circle of light or state out loud that this is a safe space for opening and healing. Call the energies of the four directions of east, south, west and north, or however you like to create awareness of the sacred.

Invocations: Calling on Higher Energies

Do an invocation internally, and also out loud as desired, of Divine energy. We invoke the energy of the Divine Mother Goddess, or the Divine Father, to include the spiritual aspects and levels of the experience, and also to help the therapist have a sense of channeling energies larger than their small self. The therapist/priestess (a trained person is called a Mamadevi or Papadeva) opens her/his self to be a channel for nurturing and healing for the receiver.

You might call in the presence of your teachers and guides, or of archetypes of the God or Goddess that you relate to, or power animals, angels, etc. You might imagine opening to your own sacred self.

The Purpose or Main Intention

This is the main reason why the ritual has been created. Whatever the purpose is, you do that work now. In Heartbeat sessions, this step consists of the Cradling and perhaps Suckling.

Closing-Release the Sacred Space

Bring the event to a close and give thanks, release all the energies you invoked. Open the circle by stating that the sacred space has been ended and the intent is to return to normal consciousness. In a Heartbeat session, this consists of bringing them back out of the hypnotic state and back into moving their body. Be sure to allow plenty of time for this step.

Clearing Afterward

We covered clearing in Chapter 8 in detail. Do some aura combing, grounding, visualizing light, hand sweeps, or just washing your hands

Be sure to clear your own energy and separate out from the client so you do not carry away the energy they let go of in their session.

Chapter 10.
Reclaiming Our Breasts

Emotions About Breasts

It seems like we are completely obsessed with breasts in our western culture. Breasts are displayed in many advertisements, and a lot of male attention is focused on breasts. Sex sells things, and breasts are the easiest things for the conscious triggering of our sexual patterns used by the advertising industry. The word "tittilation" expresses this well. Women spend a lot of time and money trying to get their breasts to look "good" according to the cultural standard, which apparently means that all breasts should be large, firm and upright.

One male student said "A lot of my sexual energy is spend simply trying to get access to some breasts". Many women also have a strong attraction to breasts, especially if they were not breastfed. Unless they are lesbian or bisexual, however, they do not have access to touching another woman's breasts. A look in any sex toy shop will show that there are many, many images of penises and breasts, but not many of yonis or vulvas. That is a curious phenomenon. Perhaps the breasts seem less frightening or intensely sexual than a vulva?

Perhaps part of this intense interest is leftover frozen needs from lack of breastfeeding. Breastfeeding is both hugely important in meeting our early needs for closeness, as we have seen, and is also inherently pleasurable for the mother and infant. It is often sexually stimulating for the mother, if not consciously then it is felt in generating oxytocin and other pleasure hormones. It is a beautiful and intimate activity, and we miss it deeply if we do not have it as infants.

The whole breastfeeding experience has strong influence on our emotions. How your mother felt about her breasts, and about breastfeeding you, if she did, got communicated to you as a baby. The whole process of weaning is also important. Spend some time scanning your memories, and if you don't know what happened, it might be interested to question your mother. You can also just guess and "make up a story" and often that will bring memories up from the subconscious.

Understanding the emotions around suckling is important and affects many areas of our later relationships. It can show up as and oral obsession with food, chewing gum, or smoking. It is often linked to feeling abandoned and unlovable, and mistrust of others. If you find yourself mindlessly reaching for something to put in your mouth, or chewing on fingernails, you can suspect that there are early needs that were not met.

Frozen needs, as we have seen create a strange mix of both fear and desire. We can find ourselves either being pulled to want something all the time, or to be avoiding it all the time. We avoid it for the same reason we avoid any triggering event; because it reminds us of our hurts. These feelings can come up in these sessions.

Practice: Your Relationship with Breasts
In pairs, do a short listening session trade. Pair up with someone of the same gender. How do you feel about breasts? Yours and others? What were you told by others about breasts?

Breasts as Sacred Objects

When we come into our power and pride in our inner Divine Feminine, we can get in touch with the beauty and magnetism of our breasts. They are more than just objects of desire or milk generators. They are highly magnetic and are connected to expressing our heart energy. They are really fountains of love. They are soft and benign sources of nourishment, radiating benevolence. Tuning in to the power of the breasts, and owning them as sacred objects can be very liberating.

Men can also offer suckling if they are comfortable with their own inner Goddess or mothering energy. Just focus on sending love from the heart. Anyone without breasts can offer nurturing cradling and a client might choose to use a pacifier or a thumb to suck on. A lot of us used thumbs for comfort for years, so if you can let yourself get past the embarrassment, using a thumb for oral stimulation is great.

Most of the rest of this chapter is aimed at preparing women to offer suckling as part of therapy.

Women: Nurture Our Breasts

One great way to reclaim your breasts is to practice massaging and loving them. Practicing breast massage techniques with your favorite oil brings new life and energy to the breasts. There are many health benefits, including the movement of lymph toxins and rejuvenating the tissues, which otherwise do not get much exercise. Massage cleanses, tones, rejuvenates and beautifies your breasts. It improves the flow of fresh nutrients, blood, and oxygen.

Practice it for 5 to 15 minutes at least every other day for best results, but any of it helps. A good time to practice is first thing in the morning or just before bed. Make all movements gentle and slow. Warm enough oil in your hands for a smooth glide. You can add your own variations to these suggestions. Breathe deeply and slowly while you massage. Also use visualizations, such as sending love and soothing affection to your breasts. If you like, squeeze your vaginal muscles at the same time, and imagine bringing the warm sexual energy up. Taoists practices teach these techniques, so study that tradition for more details. See the References section for excellent books.

Breast Massage

Circling - Place your hands on your breasts and massage them in both directions, 36 times each way, beginning with in and up- out and down, using firm pressure. The go the other way: out and up, in and down. Your hands are moving in opposite circles during this practice, in other words, one is going clockwise, and the other counterclockwise, and then reversing. If you don't have time to do 36 repetitions, do at least 9 each direction. In between, rest and hold your cupped breasts in each hand, and focus on breathing deeply and slowly.

Stroking Out/Milking - Do this 3 or more times per breast: One hand cups the top of the breast, the other cups the lower. Start at the base of the breast and pull out toward the nipple, imagining that you are clearing away any unwanted energy or stagnation. Then move your hands so that you are on the sides of the breast, and stroke out 3 times.

Stroking In - Start at the nipple and stroke toward the body in opposite directions. Continue the strokes, this time stroking out to the sternum and the side of your body. Eventually stroke your way around the entire breast. Make these strokes light and slow. Breathe!

Twisting - Do this 3 or more times per breast: Slowly and gently twist each breast, first in clock-wise, then anti-clockwise direction. Be gentle with the breasts, as the tissue is delicate.

Kneading - Knead both breasts like you would knead bread, gently lifting, squeezing, and pressing them.

Jiggling - Cup each breast in your hands and jiggle them for a minute or two. It feels great!

Finger Tip Massage - Put your fingertips lightly on the outside of the nipples and begin massaging in gentle small circles, as though you are doing a breast check. Progress around the whole breast in outward moving spirals. Finish with light fingertip strokes around the outside of the nipples.

Cupping - Placing your palms on both breasts, gently compress them toward the chest wall. Hold them a firmly and think of how much you appreciate them. Focus on breathing slowly in and out, squeezing the pelvic floor. Imagine unconditional love flowing from your heart into the breasts.

Practice: Shared Breast Massage
In pairs of women, trade giving breast massage, using your hands to nurture each other. Or trade with someone without breasts and enjoy having your breasts nurtured in a non-sexual context.

Offering the Breast in Therapy

If the only time you have ever had your breasts touched was during sex, or by a tiny child, then it might feel strange to let an adult touch them, especially if they are not your lover. It helps a lot if you are in your own power and thinking of your breasts as sacred channels of love. Think of yourself as providing a gift to someone who was not given the gift earlier in their life. It is a change to fill in a missing piece.

If you are not interested in imagining you are the Divine Mother, simply think of yourself as a substitute good mama. Focus on reaching for their inner infant, who is the one who really needs the experience you are offering. Be willing to give them your breast for a little while, and for them to have the feeling that it belongs to them by right. This is what infants feel, that the breasts are made for them, and should be always available to them.

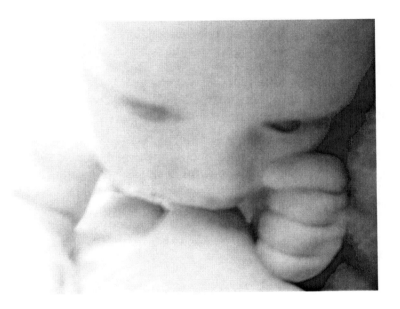

If the receiver is your lover, it could be challenging to stay focused on the therapeutic intent, and not get distracted into a lovemaking session. It can be very nice to include a little suckling therapy into lovemaking. Just be clear on what your intent is. If you are really going for healing early infant distress, then stay focused on being in mother and child roles.

When you are giving a session, and you have done a regression and already played around with baby sounds, mama messages etc, then you might choose to offer the breast at some point. This needs to be intentional, because you will need to shift positions from the heartbeat cradling to a lower position of their head. It should be discussed before you start the session if you intend to include suckling. Also, it is best to do the whole session with no top on, if you intent to suckle.

Shift their head slowly down into the crook of your arm. Hopefully this can happen without too much interruption of the hypnotic trance state. Encourage them to stay relaxed and let you move them.

Start with touching your breast to the face, using your hand to move it around softly on the face. Encourage them to pat and nuzzle and play with the breast, maybe patting it with their hand or rubbing it on their face. Encourage them to think of the breast as belonging to them.

Then invite them to nuzzle and explore with their face, "borrow" your breast, and at some point suckle. Keep talking to them as though they are an infant. If they suck too hard, tell them softly to be gentle. The problem with adults suckling is they have teeth! Since many people got weaned suddenly the first time the bit their mother, be aware of gentleness in how you guide the suckling.

Also be gentle when it is time for them to stop. You may need to stop because of time or because you don't feel comfortable continuing. Always stop giving if you feel uncomfortable. Just let them know that it is time to let go soon and let the infant self "go to sleep". Give them a minute or two warning. Then take them into another relaxation. A suggested monologue for this process is found in Chapter 12. under *Suckling Invitation.*

Chapter 11.
Challenges in the Therapy Process

Letting Yourself Be Little

How wonderful it feels to just drop all the effort, and all the adult concerns and worries, and just let yourself be little. To trust and totally relax and be taken care of, is something most of us crave. But it is not so easy to do, after all the conditioning and hurts around having to be tough, to take care of ourselves, and to not trust others who may disappoint us. All the embarrassment about acting like a child, and showing our weaknesses and pain to another person get in the way of just letting go. It takes courage and a strong intention to let ourselves curl up into that little whimpering infant and really act it out.

Yet is we can have that courage, and really go after the deepest places that feel like we will never survive feeling them, we emerge free and more alive. We need to take that magical inner journey and come to the aid of the lost child. Asking permission on the adult ego self is a very important step, so that it is acknowledged that the hurt and needy self who emerges in the session is not the only self. And it is also important to transition back out of the inner child, so that we are not stuck with our attention in that self after the session.

Letting Yourself Be Loved

If we have had experiences where others were not loving us well, or reluctant to love us, or were attacking us, we carry deep feelings of being unlovable. Getting through these feelings is like pushing through dense grasses trying to go forward into intimacy. Even with a counselor there, who is willing to be present and loving, it can be hard to let in the love that is available. The counselor is providing a lot of good counteractions by being physically close, gentle and attentive. Yet still doubts will arise, and thoughts like "this is not real", "this is silly" or "I wonder if they will get bored with giving to me?"

Whatever thought or feelings you had in past experiences will undoubtedly arise as you attempt to get close to people now. Inner blocks can be as subtle as suddenly spacing out, or going to sleep, whenever intimacy is happening. If someone is praising us, we might brush it aside rather that really letting it in. If someone is really loving us, we might feel mistrustful and wonder if they are trying to get something from us.

All of these old feelings are to be welcomed and studied, because they reveal the shape of the old hurts. In these sessions, let yourself be loved as much as possible, and be honest about the thoughts and feelings that arise as you attempt to do that. When you are in the regressed trance state, you may not feel like talking, but you may still notice the feelings. You can speak them aloud in the debriefing after the session. Or you may just say a few words while being cradled, such as "Do you really love me?" or "Tell me how you want to be close to me".

What If I Have No Partner?

What about someone who has no friends or lovers willing to do this practice, who wants to work with healing this way?

Solo therapy work can be very powerful, and means you will need to be more focused and skilled. It can be a great practice in self-loving. You might want to use props like big pillows or blankets to help you feel wrapped up, and nipple substitutes.

You can learn to put yourself into a light trance using recordings or just visualization. Making your own recordings of the visualizations in the next chapter is a very strong technique, and helps you relax and stay focused during the session.

If you want to hear someone else's voice, get a copy of the "Holding You Close" CD, listed in final pages of the book. It offers a full guided Heartbeat Session, with relaxing music and both male and female voices. It is also useful for hearing with a friend just holding you, if they do not know how to do a full session.

The advantage to working alone is that you can do it as much as you want, any time you want. People have reported using the CD repeatedly and having strong healing emotional experiences. The disadvantage is you do not have the warm presence of another person.

Attachments, Rejection, Projection

These are some of the most common feelings that come up in relationships. Attachments are really common when things are going well. Finally, here is someone who we can share love with, who is enjoying us and is giving us what we crave! We want to stay with them all the time, and certainly do not want to do anything to lose this wonderful source of love.

The level of complete attachment that a baby has, which is based on survival needs, is far heavier than what is normal between adults. If your infantile needs are triggered, and are allowed to run your behavior, they may quickly strangle a love relationship. Adults usually want a certain amount of personal freedom, and the relationship between a mother and infant is not about freedom. If your infant self has identified someone as a potential parent substitute, it will cling for dear life.

This often brings about a situation where to other person feels controlled and pushes away, bring about a feeling of rejection for the clingy child. Since we got lots of messages about how bad it was to be clingy and needy, (even thought that is perfectly natural for a young child), it re-enforces the old hurts. Feeling rejected, we pull away and it makes it even harder to open up and reach out again. The inner child becomes terrified to show itself. Clients are vulnerable to feeling rejected after sessions, so the giver should be careful to be calm, centered and loving.

Transference and How to Avoid It

When the inner child has identified an object of affection and parental substitute, it will project upon that persona all the qualities that it wished to have from the original parent. How many times have we watched our friends fall in love, and they seem to be in a completely unrealistic fog, believing that their lover is perfect? It appears to be

101

some kind of restimulated temporary insanity, which usually wears off after around three to six months. Then they discover their lover has patterns and personality quirks, and the real relationship work begins.

Being a parent substitute is exactly what we are doing in sessions, only consciously and with agreement. So it is really important to be aware that the baby self may experience this latching on to the therapist, which is called transference. The client is likely to project unrealistic beliefs onto the therapist.

Sometimes, especially when you are starting out working with a new person, you may find that you have vague feelings about them, even if you do not know them at all. These feelings may be positive or negative. It often happens that a counselor reminds us of someone that we knew in the past, and we may be reacting to them as though they are the other person from our past.

When we are role-playing being someone's parent, we are inviting the child to allow being nurtured by the counselor. However we are doing this for a short and specified period of time. It is important to help the child self understand that this is a special moment. Although the counselor is really there, giving real love and attention, they are not actually a parent and the client is not actually a child. The experience will be over and life will go on.

Clearing up this confusion and making a clear distinction between the two people, who are in fact very different, will help greatly.

If you find yourself feeling attached to the counselor afterward, spend some time owning your space, separating your energy and thinking of the ways that they are different from your parents. Generally after sessions, it is good for both people to ground and separate.

As a counselor, if this is a persistent problem, you can help by asking the receiver:

> Who do I remind you of?
>
> -How am I like him/her?
>
> -How and I different from him/her?
>
> -How did you feel toward him/her?

102

Integrity As A Therapist

Be aware that giving in this way puts the other person is a very vulnerable, and also programmable place. We are using many things that take them into altered states to provide help and healing. Make sure you are not giving them programs they did not choose. They are the ones designing the messages they want to hear, and designing the session. You are there to support them in going the way they want to go, not the way you think they should.

If you are giving a session to someone who is not your lover, and they suddenly decide that now you should be lovers, be aware that this is probably not a rational desire coming from the adult self. It is a magnificent opportunity, however, to work with deep frozen needs.

If you have the skill and centeredness to be present while someone tells you of their longing to be close and attached to you, and you do not act on it, this can be life changing for them. Stay loving and present, and thank them for the compliment of their desire, but do not get pulled into trying to meet the frozen needs. Listen to how much they want you and long for deep love, and guide the energy back to the early memories, with questions about how this feeling has come up in the past. This is a huge service and can help people be free of persistent old needs.

I was gifted with this service by one of my lovers, who was excellent at channeling loving presence, yet was not interested in an attached partnership. My inner child went crazy obsessing about him for several months, missing him and going through all the feelings of longing, desire, rejection and anger. Luckily I knew what was going on and could recognize it as a triggered pattern. He was also trained as a healer and counselor, so he was able to listen to me as I cried and raged. He gently helped remind me that these were old feelings about my father. After a period of time, my strong feelings abated and I wondered why I was so interested in a partnership with him, since our needs in life obviously did not match. All my relationships with men were transformed and greatly improved after that. We are still dear friends and I will always be grateful for that process.

Your Sexual Feelings as a Therapist

Be aware that you, as a giver, are also getting needs met for closeness during these sessions. Almost no one has managed to satisfy all needs for closeness. It is fine to use the sessions for this and enjoy them, as long as you are freely giving and receiving and not using them to control the other person in any way.

Watch out for your own need for praise and adoration, and watch your own pulls to initiate sexual activity with someone who is trusting you deeply. It is easy to be confused because of all the pain we have had. Resist the pull to explore sex with a client who is not already your lover. Doing so is rich material for growth.

Your sexual feelings may arise while being suckled, since the nipples are directly connected with the clitoris energetically, as most women have discovered. Also many hormones and other brain chemicals are released as your breasts are suckled, all of which have a very healing effect you. Enjoy the aroused feelings, and keep breathing the energy up through your heart and out through your arms to them. Pulling the energy upward will spread it around your body and you may feel very good and energized afterward. If you are the kind of person who has energetic orgasms easily, just let them happen and enjoy them, and stay focused on channeling the energy out to the receiver.

The sexual energy acts as a supercharger for the love energy, and makes it more potent and magnetic. Think of it as pure life force energy, and don't take it personally. It does not mean anything in your relationship with this other person, necessarily. It just means that a lot of life and magic is flowing.

If you can't feel comfortable with the sexual feelings that may be arising, consider what is coming up for you and work with it in your own sessions, with someone else.

Generally, it is best to not engage in sexual activity any time near a full session that you have shared with a lover. Let some time pass in between.

If you are already making love and you spontaneously integrate a little cradling or suckling, that is a different situation. Cradling is very nice for afterglow, and helps the brain to create bonding hormones that ameliorate the reactivity phase after people have orgasms. There is very interesting research about the brain chemistry that happens during love and sex. One book about this is *Peace Between the Sheets*, by Marnia Robinson. Other information about this can be found in Mantak Chia's many book on Taoist practices.

Blessing Each Other

Even though there are challenges in this kind of emotional work, the rewards are great. For those who are really committed to their own healing and recovery from the programming and pain from this culture, trading healing is a really accessible way to do so. For many people trading this will be the only way to get this experience, because it will not be available from professionals.

We trade healing and both of us are enriched and nurtured. We trade and it affirms our equality and our connection. We take turns being the Divine Parent and the Magical Child, and coming back into our functional adult self. All of our selves are acknowledged and fed, and can come into a better integration inside.

Appreciate yourself and your friends for learning this and for having the courage to show up and reach out for closeness. Appreciate yourself for being here in this world, now, and deciding that love is the way. Feel free to share this with whoever is interested.

May all beings be free, happy, nurtured, and well.

Chapter 13.
Resources for Use in Heartbeat Nurturing Therapy Sessions

Included here are outlines and text of visualizations that you can use to base your sessions on. Feel free to make up your own wording. This is just to jet your started. You can read these aloud into a recording device and use them to give yourself sessions.

Feel free to photocopy these for your own use.

Outline of a Full Sacred Nurturing Session

Use this as a reminder of the steps to the process. Keep it near you during a session.

Prepare the Room
Prepare Yourself: Practice meditation and clearing your energy

The Interview: Start by discussing these things:
> What is their birth history? Relationship with their parents? Breastfeeding experience?
> Use the interview questions, in the worksheet below.

Mama/Papa Message Design:
Ask for what they most wanted to hear from their mother/father, and write it down.
Ask how they would most **like to be touched** by their parent.

Setting intent for this session: ask them what their intent is.

Optional Purification & Blessing,
Grounding Together
Making the Container
Invocations: Calling on Higher Energies

The Basic Process:

Cradling: Invite them to put their head on your heart, OR do this after the regression. Find the most comfortable position.

Regression/ Hypnotic Induction:
> Basic guided relaxation, with deep breathing.
> Then invite them to go back in time to when they were a child, ask permission to speak to them as though they are a child now.

Optional Meditation: Meeting the God/dess
> Guide them in imagining that they are being held by the Mother goddess or Father God, totally adored by Her/Him. Speak as though the Divine voice is coming through you.

Mama/Papa Messages: Speak in your own words the messages they want to hear.
As appropriate:

Encourage the client to make baby sounds,
Speak in gibberish or other languages
Humming, toning or singing lullabies
Thumb sucking
Optional Advanced Process: Suckling
Offering the breast, nuzzling, suckling

Finishing the session

Bringing the infant back through time, growing up with the new imprints
Bringing the Divine Parent back with them more fully
Remembering all that has happened and integrating this into the adult persona
Thanking and cherishing the infant self
Drifting to sleep, letting go, laying them down
Resting time for integration, spooning

Waking up, Coming Back to Normal

Guide then in coming back to a more normal waking state, feeling refreshed and alert, remembering everything they experienced.

After the Session

Discussion and integration: How do they feel now? Anything they want to share?

Action steps: Ask them how can they include more self-nurturing in their lives? Help them brainstorm.

Release the Sacred Space:

Separate and ground yourselves.
Give thanks to the energies you called on, release of energies, send the blessings out to share with others
Imagine opening and dissolving the circle you created for healing work.
Clearing Afterward: Clear your energy in a way you choose.

Bring the attention back to normal everyday activities, such as what you will do next.

Heartbeat Nurturing Therapy- Initial Interview
Questions for writing and discussion. Use more paper if needed.

What is your birth history?   Where, how, what happened?

How was your relationship with your mother or father? Were you close or not?

What was your breast feeding experience, and night time sleep experience?

Did you have any violent experiences such as being touched in anger?

How did this affect you?

What would you have loved to get more of from your mother (or father)?

Positive Message Design:
What did you most want to hear from your mother/father?

What makes you feel most nurtured?   (What kind of touch or experience?)

Guided Deep Relaxation
by Amara Karuna

A basic guided meditation script you can start with goes as follows:

"Begin by sitting in a comfortable position or laying down. Take a moment to check that each part of your body is completely comfortable.

Now become aware of your breathing. Simply observe how you are breathing. Is it shallow or deep, quick or slow? Are you breathing through your mouth or nose? Gently breathe through your nose, and expand your belly fully, then your upper chest, for a full deep breath. Exhale through your mouth emptying your upper chest first, then your belly. Take at least 3 deep full breaths like this.

With every exhale, you become more relaxed. You feel yourself drifting, letting go, melting into the ground.

Now simply relax and breathe however and whenever you want to. You are going deeper into relaxation, becoming more relaxed than ever before.

Your attention is drawn to your feet, and you feel your toes and feet and ankles letting go, releasing all tension. A warm golden light begins to fill them from the soles of the feet, rising upward. Breathing deeply, you feel your lower legs and your knees, becoming soft and relaxed, warm and loose, filling with light.

The warm golden light fills your upper legs, your buttocks, and your pelvis, relaxing all the muscles and tendons, releasing all the organs. Breathing deeply, your lower back and abdomen fill with golden warmth and love, sending affectionate, smiling energy to all the cells, and blood begins to circulate more freely in the soft, relaxed tissues.

Taking a slow delicious breath, your middle back and solar plexus relaxes, filling your liver, stomach, spleen and all the area with love and warm energy. every breath helps you let go even deeper, while you stay alert and present, hearing my voice, able to remember everything that happens while you relax.

As you breathe in the golden light of love, your chest and upper back fills with new energy and lets go, then both shoulders, and your neck, are becoming soft and relaxed, warm and loose, filling with light. Your heart and lungs become open and soft, happy and safe.

As you go ever deeper, the warm energy flows into your upper arms, elbows, lower arms, wrists and hands. Light pours out through your fingertips, carrying away any energies you no longer need.

112

Your facial muscles and your scalp muscles completely let go and relax, your jaw letting go and opening, as you take a slow deep breath. Every breath helps you let go even deeper into relaxation, while you stay alert and present with this moment. Your eyes are full of warm golden light, and your head sinks down into the earth. Your brain and ears and neck are relaxed and full of warmth.

You can feel your entire body now completely relaxed, and full of healing warm light, feeling loved and cared for, floating in an ocean of love."

Add in a regression, the therapeutic inner infant work or other meditation at this point, if you like. Or do the awakening process.

Closing/Awakening

Do this step if you are not about to go into a longer session, and want to bring yourself back.

"Now coming back to your more normal waking state, feeling refreshed and alert, remembering everything you experienced.

Taking a breath in, start to wiggle your fingers and toes, gradually followed by your ankles and wrists. Coming back, waking up, lifting your arms and legs up and down a little. When you feel ready, move a little more and then open your eyes slowly. Take your time, stretch, roll on your side and get up whenever you feel ready."

Guided Regression To The Inner Child

by Amara Karuna © 2011

Begin with a basic guided relaxation as above, with deep breathing, for at least 5 minutes. Then cradle the person in your arms to hear the heartbeat.

Then continue with this regression:

"You can feel your entire body now completely relaxed, and full of healing warm light, feeling loved and cared for, floating in an ocean of love. See a beautiful golden light more pure than you have ever seen before surrounding your body. It is filling every inch of your body and overflowing to a few feet around you.

Now become aware that you are being drawn back through time, to send this love to times and places in your past. You begin to drift backward, watching time roll backwards as you remember things that happened last night, and during the day yesterday.

Flowing back more, you remember things that happened last week, people you saw, what you felt. And you jump backwards to last year, this same time a year ago, and notice what you were doing then. You send some love and light to who you were then, and keep going backward, as you take a deep breath and relax."

(The following ages are optional- you can go right to the infant if you like. Include all the ages if you have a long time.)

"Now you find yourself carried back to when you were 20 years old. Notice what you looked like, what your energy was like, what you were doing. What were you learning about then? Greet your 20 year old self and send some light and love and blessing.

Again you are carried back in time, and you see yourself at 10 years old. Where are you? what are you doing? How do you feel? Greet your 10 year old self, and send some blessing. Does this child self have a message for you now? What does the child need to hear from you? Take a deep breath and relax, staying present and aware, remembering all that happens as you journey.

Letting yourself be carried back even farther as you breathe deeply, and you find yourself at 5 years old. Notice how your body is so much smaller and younger. Your arms and legs are very short. How do you feel? What is happening? Greet your 5 year old self and ask if there is any message they have for you. Ask if there is anything they want from you. Send light and love to the child.

Allowing yourself to relax even deeper, you find yourself as a small infant. Your body is very, very small, your skin very soft, your

114

fingers tiny and delicate. You do not have to do anything, since you cannot move your body well yet.

You can make sounds and communicate what you want... make some baby sounds now. Experiment with the sounds you can make, with total freedom. Make babbling sounds, and hunger sounds, and impatient sounds."

Meeting the Mother Goddess (Optional meditation)

Or you can meet the Divine Father here. The wording can be changed to be first person, as in "You are my child..."

"As you lay there in your infant body, feel a huge warmth surround you, and feel as though very large warm arms are enfolding you. You are held close next to soft and full breasts, and you hear a heart beating. You know that you are cherished as a most precious child, a jewel, a treasure. The mother goddess wants all good things for you, wants you to have every desire fulfilled, every comfort, always surrounded by love and abundance. Breathe deeply and allow this generous loving energy to come into you. More than you ever have before. Let her nurture you. You deserve it. You are her child, her own creation.

She offers you her huge warm breast, and you open your mouth and feel the sweetest energy in the world coming in to you, filling your heart and belly. It is pure and clean, and totally satisfying, like nectar. She has more than enough, and she wants to give you as much as you want. Let yourself take everything you want, as much as you want. She has more than you could possibly every need, to take all that you need. It is your right to be filled, to be whole, to be loved."

(Personal Mama Messages may happen here).

(Suckling or nuzzling may happen here).

Suckling Invitation (Optional)

The Mother Goddess says: "Here you are, precious little one. Take all that you want. I have enough for you, and enough for everyone. I have brought you here into life, and I will feed you and care for you and keep you safe. This is here all for you."

At the end of the suckling time, She says: "I have fed until you feel warm and full, and now it is time to relax and let the infant fall asleep, satisfied and full. In a moment you can let the nipple fall away, and you roll gently to the side. Then we will bring you back trough time, remembering everything and bringing me with you."

Meditation- Meeting the Inner Divine Father

"As you lay there in your infant body, feel a huge warmth surround you, and feel as though very large warm arms are enfolding you. You are held close next to a strong muscular chest, and you hear a heart beating. You might feel the hairs on his chest and arms.

You know you are completely safe. You know that you are cherished as a most precious child, a jewel, a treasure. The father wants all good things for you, and wants to be close to you. He wants for you to be protected, and always surrounded by love and abundance.

Breathe deeply and allow this generous loving energy to come into you. More than you ever have before. Let him nurture you. You deserve it. You are his child, his own creation, and he is proud of you. You can completely relax and let go, and he will take care of you."

(Personal Papa Messages may happen here, for example: "You are my precious little one", "I am proud of you", "I want to spend lots of time with you", "I am so glad you are my baby" and "You bring me joy".)

Coming Back Home

After the Inner child Regression, let the client down slowly from the position of being cradled. Do it slowly as you would a baby.

Then continue with this meditation:

"Thank the Infant self. Greet your infant self from your higher self, and send light and love. What do you want to tell this infant? What does the infant want to say to you? Take the infant in your arms and bring them back with you through time. Bring the Divine parent energy with you as well, filling up the years with the feeling of loving support and connection.

Come back to the 5 year old, and imagine what it would have been like if this supportive parenting energy was there when you were five. Invite them to come back also, bring them with you through time.

Stop in time for the 10 year old, and imagine if that child had all the loving support they needed. What would their life have been like? Invite them to come with you forward in time.

Gather them all with you as you come back forward in time, meeting the 20 year old, and all the years in between, each one a part of you, weaving them all together in one long strand of light, bringing them back here to this moment, to this room where you are relaxed and safe.

All of them can live inside your heart, welcome and honored, as parts of your story and your path. They can live there with the loving parent who created them. Remembering all that has happened and integrating it into the adult persona.

Imagine all your past hurts, physical problems and mental barriers being drawn into the light where they dissipate forever. (Long pause for visualization) Picture the golden light from your center outwards. "

Roll the receiver onto their side gently. Spend some time spooning them from behind, and letting them rest with no sound from you. After a time, help them come back out.

"Now coming back to your more normal waking state, feeling refreshed and alert, remembering everything you experienced.

Taking a breath in, start to wiggle your fingers and toes, gradually followed by your ankles and wrists. Coming back, waking up, lifting your arms and legs up and down a little.

When you feel ready, move a little more and then open your eyes slowly. Take your time, stretch, roll on your side and get up whenever you feel ready."

Appendixes

Appendix 1. Counseling Actual Children

Respect is the most important thing to offer a young person. Especially respect their feelings, even if they seem to be silly or irrational to you. Children will often react strongly to something that is relatively minor, as an "excuse" to work on deeper things that are really hurting them.

Watch out for the tendency to demean, discount, disrespect, laugh at and otherwise treat young people as though they are not as important or intelligent as adults. Involve the young person in all decisions about their life. Explain to them what is happening when they are curious. Look for ways that you can empower them rather than do things for them. Include them in conversations when in a group, and ask their opinions respectfully. Adults often laugh when a child acts powerfully and says what they think. What would you feel if you were laughed at in this way?

Also, avoid condescending, cooing "baby talk". This immediately gives a message that the child is not worthy or capable of respectful communication. What would it imply if you talked to an adult that way? Just talk to them like normal people, in words they can understand. Listen closely, avoid interrupting and adding, explaining and advising or directing the conversation.

Make sure you don't complain about young people when they can hear. It is common for a group of adults to sit around complaining about children in very demeaning tones. We tend to act as though the young people are not even there, even though they may be hearing every word. Keep this kind of clienting for your sessions, or at least away from young ones.

Special time is a way of counteracting the oppression with listening, following and playing with the child.

Adults are often distracted and interrupted when they are with young people, so children cannot count on getting adult attention consistently. Babies may not understand what an interruption is, and from their point of view, the adult attention may disappear without warning, at any moment. This lack of secure attention means that children do not often bring up deep distresses for discharge. They give up on getting attention after a while.

Adults can assist their healing process by making regular predictable times to give the child attention, with no interruptions. Use this special time to do whatever the young person wants, follow their lead and they will eventually bring up the distress. Start with short time periods at first, if it's hard for you.

When counseling them, swallow your "adult pride" and get rid of any feelings of "they can't talk to me that way." They will often need to be angry, rebellious and disrespectful as clients, in order to discharge the constant oppression and powerlessness they experience as young people. You can clearly distinguish between what is OK in session and out of session.

Children who get special time are more able to discharge around the adults in general, even outside the special time. They may not use the special time to release feelings, especially at first. Often they will use it in ways to test the adult and push the limits. Like they may want to play in the mud, especially if they know you have a pattern about getting dirty. Giving them the power to lead is a very good counteraction to the powerless feelings all children have. If you can go along with it, it can prove to the child that you will pay attention even when things get rough. (Of course, interrupt them if they are being destructive or hurtful.)

Let them win whenever possible. Let them dominate you, push you over, direct you, insult you, etc. It is important not to play a miserable victim in this kind of roleplaying, as they may worry they are really hurting you. Instead play either a cheerful victim "Oh dear, you knocked me over again! What shall I do?" or play a very exaggerated (so they know it is a game) version of an oppressive adult; "You can't knock me over! I'm a big mean grown up! You have to do whatever I say!" And then fall over with a great scream of mock dying. This helps them discharge feelings of powerlessness, and they will often laugh for a long time and want to do it over and over.

As parents, we want to help our children discharge, and can come across looking worried and concerned. A worried counselor will not help anyone feel safe. Instead of paying attention to fixing the child's distress, spend your time paying attention to how delightful they are as people. It is often more important to young people that you want to be close to them than your wanting them to discharge. When they feel enough attention available to them, they will discharge.

120

The key to counseling children is to go back and work on your own childhood distress. Often the feeling that comes up is "I never got attention like this!" "They get so much more than I did, and still they want more!" It is very important to spend time in your own sessions on what was hard for you during the playtime. Even what seems like small petty triggers are very important to work on. Few things are more restimulating than counseling children, when you first begin. It will bring up every pattern around your own childhood, as so is an incredible opportunity to clear yourself. Be sure to get support for yourself! Counseling young people can be difficult because they are not as careful with you as a counselor. They will think nothing of insulting and rejecting you, as a way to release their own feelings of being insulted and rejected. It is sure to bring up your chronic material!

Especially, work on what gets in the way of you being silly and playful. Counseling children requires absolute flexibility and lack of pretense and pride. Be willing to play a fool and a clown, to get dirty and take insults cheerfully. Also, work on any discomfort around physical closeness and being able to do lots of cuddling, wrestling, pillow fighting, etc.

COUNSELING ON DEMAND

One of the tricky things about counseling children is that they often demand it at a moment's notice. This requires a great amount of flexibility and attention from the adult.

If there is a lot of safety at home, the young people may dramatize and ask for attention a lot. All acting out is a request for attention so the child can discharge hurts. No one acts "bratty" for the fun of it, or asks for more attention than they really need. They just need a lot! Much more than one or two adults can give. An African saying is "It takes a village to raise a child." Isolation from adequate resources of attention is a primary hurt in our culture.

The child always deserves attention. But you may not have it at that moment, and it may not be possible to find another adult to help. If you can calmly explain that the child's feelings and needs are OK, but you are not able to fill them now and tell them the reason, this is very helpful.

One of the worst parts of being in a situation of limited resource is that we are often made to feel guilty for needing what we need. We are shamed and even abused for asking for more. Soon our needs become frozen into distress patterns that seem like bottomless pits, as the recording of "I don't have enough attention" gets played over and over. In an ideal world, everyone would be able to release a hurt completely as soon as they got it, with lots of loving people around to listen. We can work toward that ideal by developing a wide circle of friends and counselors for ourselves and our children.

Appendix 2. Counseling on Food and Eating

WAYS TO COUNSEL ON FOOD & EATING- Suggested directions

Give yourself a lot of slack and appreciation during a session. It is a very deep and heavy topic, working with basic early needs. Working on food can sink you into a hopeless feeling, so work on the earliest memories, and use fun directions. Always appreciate and adore yourself the way you are right now. Contradict the shame and blame.

Say "I love my magnificent body" and list everything you like about it. Looking in a mirror is a good way to do this.

Try fasting one meal or one day, and get sessions! What feelings come up if you let yourself be hungry?

Tell you counselor about all the forbidden foods you would eat if you didn't have to worry about weight or health.

When do you eat when you are not hungry? Why?

Play with your food- have a food fight (great for "mess distress" too!)

How did your eating habits change when you moved away from your parents' house?

Suck your thumb or a bottle- or just think about doing it (a great way to discharge embarrassment!)

Confront your issues around feeling childlike and needy. We were often made to feel our needs were not OK. Let yourself feel needy. Have your counselor parent you the way it should have been. (Say "I need you" or "I want my momma!" If it feels safe enough)

Use all the standard ways to work on addictions:

Scan early memories of food and eating

Scan how your parents acted about food, and about weight

Get to know the addiction- watch how you feel before you do it, while doing it, and afterwards.

122

Think about your emotional attachments to certain foods. Which foods would you most hate to give up? Which food will you never eat? What are your earliest memories of those foods?

Say goodbye to the food you are addicted to.

Bring food to session, pay attention to how you feel as you eat it or think about eating it. Feel the desire, slow down and notice how it tastes, notice your hunger level. Tell your counselor whatever comes up.

Eating with loving attention on you will contradict the shame. Have the counselor tell you how perfect you are while you eat forbidden foods.

Brainstorm about all the things you could do, other than eat, when you have a strong emotion come up. For example, when you are lonely and you need attention--- you could call a friend, go out to some group event, call a counselor, or?

Make an arrangement with several counselors that you can call for minis when you are feeling a craving. Line up support.

What other activities nourish you emotionally, besides food? Try doing them more often.

Appendix 3. Counseling on Closeness and Touch

-It is easier to counsel on this with more than one counselor, such as in a three-way session, which avoids the restimulation of fear of sexual feelings.

-Say to your counselor: "Now we are going to be really close." What comes up?

-How does it feel to give touch? Talk about it.

-Ask for the touching you want in session- try being massaged, being held or cuddled, getting a long hug.

-It is important for the counselor to assure the client they want to give to them. Insist on giving a long time, or beg them to let you hug them.

What would you find deeply satisfying for other people to do for you, in terms of closeness and non-sexual touch?

Survivors of sexual abuse may want the counselor to be sensitive to their boundaries, and back off when asked. They may need to feel safe to know that they can say no and control the touching. Good direction : Beg to get close to them, and let them say "No!" and push you away.

Appendix 4. Training for Priest/ess Therapists
by Amara Karuna

If you want to be teaching people to do this, feel free. Teach your lover, teach your friends, or teach classes. The more people who are assisting each other in this way, the better. We hope it spreads widely and is useful to all. We request that if you want to teach the skill as a class, you will have taken a training class in the process first, and will practice it quite a bit, and have many of your own sessions.

No payment is needed to use the name Heartbeat Nurturing or the process, however it is required that you register with us, so we can know who is teaching and representing the work. Please let me know if you are doing so, by emailing me or becoming a member of our teacher's forum, where we can exchange information and consult with each other.

We want to maintain a high quality and integrity level in our teachers. We will also maintain a place for clients to post their feedback on teachers, so that if someone is using it in a way that is not in harmony with our intentions, others will be able to hear about it.

If you want to take this process, call it something else, and adapt it in your way, that is fine. In that case you are not required to register with us. However it would be wonderful to network with whoever is doing anything similar, so we encourage you to contact us. We can link to you on our web site. **See www.heartbeatnurturing.com.**

Outline of Training Plan

This is an outline for thoroughly training people to give this work. Adapt it as needed. This outline covers a 24 hour training that lasts for 4 classes, with each class being one six hour day. The wording and class is designed for women, however you can adapt it.

This can also be taught in shorter, day long classes, to people who already have some of the basic training, such as peer counselors or other therapists. In shorter trainings, the focus is more on giving people the experience of a session, rather that teaching them how to do it later for others. They can be led through a session trade by the teacher, and this is much easier than the process of teaching skills

It is useful to give copies of this book as part of a complete training, so that study can happen at home after the classes. It is also really important to assist the students in setting up sessions to practice outside of class.

Introductory Class #1 -6 hours
Included in this class are these topics:

Basics of Emotional Release work- Creating Safety
Healing process of discharging emotional pain
Ways we have been trained to hold back feeling
        Holding Space and staying centered
        Re-imprinting and Counteraction
Topic specific: Why birth and infancy is so important in life patterning
        Inner Selves work- Younger, Adult, Higher

Practice: Permissive counseling, what to do, what not to do as a counselor
Handouts: Basic counseling, Permissive counseling, what to do, what not to do
----

Basics of Hypnotic Induction and Regression
        Use of vocal tone and pacing
        Guiding Deep relaxation
        Giving a guided meditation- working with visual, emotional, tactile, hearing oriented people
        Trance and suggestibility

Meeting the Younger Self

Theory: Younger self as the gateway to the Divine, Magical child. Three self connections: Adult, Child and Higher self

Oppression of children and ageism. Lack of support for parents and children, society devaluing being childlike and playful.
Brainstorm: What are children naturally like?
Accessing the inner infant- imagery, sounds, movement, emotion

Practice:
Basic relaxation induction and regression of the students into the Younger self, and back out, going through ages 20, 10, 5, infant. Bringing light to the ages, honoring them as divine, asking the ages 5 and infant if they have a message, or lesson.
Handout: Sample inner child regression, Young people's oppression
----

125

Invoking the Goddess Within

Aspects of the Goddess: Maiden, Mother, Queen, Crone, Protectress
Practice: Walk around the room as though you are each of those aspects, how does it feel?
Discussion: which one feels more easy and familiar? Which is harder?

Tuning to the Mother- accessing Her
Discussion in group: What is mothering energy?
Mini session listening trade for 10-15 minutes each: How were you mothered? How open are you to being mothered now?
        What was their birth experience, breast feeding experience, and night time sleep experience?

Fill out Interview form individually

Channeling the Goddess- Getting out of the Way
Theory: Going into Light Trance states
        Stepping Out of the Ego self- Fana
        Using a ritual, prayer or object to help you access that energy

Practice: Meditation- Meeting the Inner Mother Goddess
        Journey to meet the perfect mother, open a door, approach her, what does she look like? Make contact, ask Her for what you most desire, open to receive more than before, ask to be Her channel, ask for a symbol, process/prayer or object to help you access Her. Sit in her lap and regress to infant, suckle on her.

Practice: Visualization
        Opening the hand chakras
        Opening the Heart Channel through the breasts and arms
        Energy Wrapping- extend chi out your arms and heart to wrap the person you are holding

Cradling Theory: Getting comfortable cradling an adult,
        Different positions,
        Energy wrapping,
        Synchronized breathing,
        Heartbeat listening
Practice basic cradling in pairs or trios for short sessions

Class #2- 6 hours

Cradling and Massage: Nurturing Touch for Healing
Theory: Basic human need for touch, unpleasant touch experiences, how we over focus on sex, how we block touch

Short mini session trade in pairs: When and how do you touch yourself? When and how did you get touched as a child?
Group discussion

Theory: Effects of touch, types of touch
Practice: touch your feet, in a businesslike way, in a nurturing way, in a sensual way

Minis: What touch makes you feel most nurtured? Ask for and receive it
Discussion in group

Songs and music, toning, vibrational healing
Theory on vibrational healing, synchronization. Sounds in the womb.
Heartbeat sounds

Practices in pairs: Toning/ improv songs, singing their name, whispering, gibberish. Try each for a few minutes.

Longer Basic Process Practice: Visualization
        Opening the hand chakras
        Opening the Heart Channel through the breasts and arms
        Goddess Energy Wrapping
Cradling; Goddess wrapping,
        synchronized breathing, Heartbeat listening
Practice basic cradling in pairs or trios with toning and stroking
----
Reclaiming our Breasts

Mini session: How do you feel about breasts? Yours and others?
Group discussion about our society's obsession about breasts

Practice: self breast massage, milking, spiraling instrokes, circles, nipples, cupping holds. Deer exercise

In pairs: giving breast massage, using hands to nurture

127

Using The Voice-

As Giver: Vocal Stroking, gentle vocal tones

Mama Messages Speaking Positive Messages that infants love to hear
Discussion: what would the Divine Mother feel about her precious
child? What would She say? channeling messages

Brainstorm in group: write down messages

Practice: personal Mama Message Design- What you most wanted to
hear from your mother, write it down.

In pairs- practice speaking the messages to each other, modulating
voice

Theory: How Affirmations work and how to phrase them- positive only
Group brainstorm affirmations: write down the ones you like best

Practice basic cradling in pairs or trios with with Mama messages

----

Class #3 – 6 hours

Elements and Importance of Ritual
Creating Sacred space: Purification & blessing, Setting intent, grounding, making the container, Invoking larger energies, closing the ritual, clearing the space and yourself.

Demonstrations or discussion:
Blessings: smudging, anointing, water blessing, crystals
Create sacred space: 4 directions, circle of light, crystals
Invocations: calling on higher energies
Closing: thanks, release of energies, open the circle
Clearing: aura combing, grounding, visualizing light, hand sweeps
Handout: sample ritual ideas

Practice: Create and perform a healing ritual for a partner right now
----

Beginning the session: the Interview
What is their birth history? Where, how, what happened?
How was their relationship with their mother?
What was their breast feeding experience, and night time sleep experience?
How did this effect them?
What would they have loved to get more of from their mother?
Mama Message Design: Asking for what they most wanted to hear from their mother, write it down.

Practices:
Students do interviews for each other
Handout: Interview form

Finishing the session- go over each step
Bringing the receiver back to Now
Drifting to sleep, letting go, laying them down
Bringing the infant back through time, growing up with the new imprints
Bringing the goddess back with them more fully

Remembering all that has happened and integrating into the adult persona
    Thanking and cherishing the Infant self
    Resting time for integration, spooning
Closing the session
    Waking up, looking around the room, present time questions
    Discussion and integration
    action steps to give to the inner child after session
    Opening the sacred circle

Using The Voice as a Client

As Receiver: Opening The Voice- Baby Power
Theory: The voice as the first power, throat chakra

Practice: vocal warm ups- random, animal, high/low, soft/loud, toning, yes/no in pairs

Theory; baby sounds
Discussion: What would babies need to say? What happened to you when you tried to communicate?

Needs and Frozen Needs: shame around needs, needs being good and normal

Practice: exploration of baby sounds laying down in a group- babbling, giggling, needy crying, angry crying, fear crying, sad crying, loud as possible

Practice in pairs mini: cradling with baby sounds, mother is very approving

Practice: give sessions of the basic process

130

Class #4 --- 6 hours

Counseling Theory: Transference- What to watch out for
Releasing physical pain
Emotional effects of anesthesia, releasing it

Offering the breast

Theory: Understanding the emotions around suckling
    Sexual associations from lack of breastfeeding
    Emotional effects—obsession with food/oral/smoking, feeling abandoned, unlovable
    Fear and desire mixed, frozen needs and how they heal

Encouraging nuzzling, touching and sucking
    Start with touching your breast to the face, using your hand to move it around softly on the face
    Then invite them to nuzzle and explore with their face, "borrow" your breast, and suckle
Discussion: your sexual feelings while being suckled

Demonstration of full session:
    Goddess invocation, Regression, Cradling, vocal stroking, nuzzling, suckling, finishing process

Practice: give sessions for at least 45 minutes per person

Follow Up:
    We recommend that you hold at least two practice sessions after the training, where people can focus on trading session. The practice times should be at least three hours long, so that people can do a session trade.

About the Author

Amara Wahaba Karuna has been teaching meditation, healing and counseling since 1985. She is a professional counselor and teacher of peer counseling. She studied and taught Re-evaluation co-counseling for five years, and created her own version of co-counseling, called Wholistic Peer Support Counseling. She also has studied tantra and sexual healing since 2003, in Hawaii. Heartbeat Therapy emerged from a combination of peer counseling and tantric healing practices.

She is also a leader of Dances of Universal Peace which are interfaith folk dances. She is the artist and creator of Karuna Arts, Inc where she sells her fabric art as multicultural prayer flags and banners.

As a singer/songwriter, she has published five CDs of her original music and dances, and has authored several books under her publishing business, Karuna Publishing. Her illustrations and photography have appeared in several books and many magazines. She is a member of an organic permaculture farm and community. She lives in Hawaii, in the lush rainforest jungle and near an active volcano.

See www.heartbeatnurturing.com

for ordering this book, DVDs and CDs which support this therapy.
Also join our forum to network with other interested people..

132

Please see www.karunapublishing.com
for more details and ordering.

Holding You Close CD
by Amara Karuna
This guided meditation offers
a full session of Heartbeat
Nurturing for use at home, alone or
with a friend.

Wholistic Peer
Support Counseling DVD
Beginning Techniques for effective
listening and helping others
when they are upset.

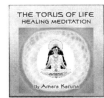

Torus of Life Healing
Meditation
by Amara Karuna
A potent movement meditation for
energizing and healing, based on
natural energy forms.

Letting The Sun Out
Mystical Poems and Photography
by Amara Karuna
Poetry in the spirit of Rumi,
exploring the ecstatic and
mysterious

It's OK to Talk About Sex
by Jane Carney Schulze
Great advice for parents
talking to children about sex

Karuna Publishing
offers several books, musical
CDs and DVDs by Amara,

See also
www.karunaarts.com
for fabric art, prayer flags and
stickers of Amara's artwork

Recommended Reading and Bibliography

Counseling & Relationships

Hendricks, Gay and Kathlyn. *At The Speed of Life, Body Centered Therapy*. New York: Bantam, 1993

Jackins, Harvey. *The Human Side of Human Beings*. Seattle: Rational Island Publishers, 1965

Jackins, Harvey. *The Fundamentals of Co-counseling Manual*. Seattle: Personal Counselors, 1962

Jackins, Harvey. *A Rational Theory of Sexuality. Pamplet*. Rational Island Publishers, 1977

Orr, Leonard. *Rebirthing in the New Age*. Trafford Publishing, 2007

Rosenburg, Marshall. *Nonviolent Communication*. Encinitas: Puddle Dancer Press, 2003

Children

Carney Schulze, Jane and Rolf. *It's OK to Talk About Sex*. Pahoa: Karuna Publishing, 2011

Hannaford, Carla. *Awakening the Child Heart*. Captain Cook: Jamila Nur Publishing, 2002

Jackins, Tim. *How Parents Can Counsel Their Children*. Seattle: Rational Island Publishers, 2000

Leboyer, Frederick. *Birth Without Violence*. Healing Arts Press, 2009

Liedloff , Jean. *The Continuum Concept: In Search Of Happiness Lost*, Da Capo Press, 1986

Leo, Pam. *Connection Parenting: Parenting Through Connection Instead of Coercion, Through Love Instead of Fear.* Wyatt-MacKenzie Publishing, 2007.

Solter, Aletha. The Aware Baby. 2001
Pearce, Joseph Chilton. Magical Child. Plume, 1992.

Thevenin, Tine. The Family Bed. Perigee Trade, 2003

Healing and Energy

Krieger, Dolores. *The Therapeutic Touch: How to Use Your Hands to Help or to Heal.* Fireside, 1979.

Wallace, Amy and Henkin, Bill. *The Psychic Healing Book.* Oakland: Wingbow Press, 1978.

Women's Practices:

Desilets, Saida. *The Emergence of the Sensual Woman.* Kihei: Jade Goddess Publishing, 2006. www.jadegoddess.com

De Vos, Minke. *Feminine Treasures.* www.silentground.com.

135